contemporary manifestations. The author moves with ease and authority through a wide range of cultural arbiters and critics of the past such as Marx, Tocqueville, Mill, Arnold, and Nietzsche.

Mr. Goodheart presents a convincing argument for the preservation of intellectual standards without denying the astringent role of criticism, radical and other, in democratic intellectual inquiry. Though he is against the politicizing of the university, he maintains that "it is not the suppression of political activity or social services that is required, but the keeping alive of a variety of political impulse, so that, among other things, the reactive and critical character of the university can be preserved and developed."

Eugene Goodheart, Professor of Literature at the Massachusetts Institute of Technology, is the author of *Cult of the Ego: The Self in Modern Literature* and *Utopian Vision of D. H. Lawrence*.

Culture and the Radical Conscience

Culture and the Radical Conscience

by Eugene Goodheart

Harvard University Press   Cambridge, Massachusetts   1973

To Alvin and Christine Kibel
and to Jessica

Acknowledgments

I am grateful to my friend Ted Weiss for his rigorously critical and yet encouraging reading of my manuscript. My thanks to my colleague Bruce Mazlish for his help and enthusiasm in reading the chapters on utopia. Joseph Frank made the necessary hard criticisms at an earlier stage of the manuscript. My profound gratitude goes to Alvin Kibel for the years of friendship and intellectual companionship. To the Christian Gauss Committee, I want to express my appreciation for the chance to formulate the arguments about utopia that were the subject of the seminars I gave at Princeton. Earlier versions of "Relevance and the Authority of Culture" and "The Humanities and Personal Knowledge" appeared in *The Centennial Review* (Fall 1968 and Fall 1969); "Cultural Radicalism in America and England" appeared, in an earlier version, in *Modern Occasions*.

E. G.

CONTENTS

Culture and the Radical Conscience

Introduction

It has become an American habit to stress the rapid changefulness of our cultural life, so that an idea or attitude scarcely achieves visibility before it is already in the process of becoming obsolete. Since much of the change has been painful, the excessive fashion-consciousness may be a mark of a compulsion to avoid painful subjects, to repress what is fundamentally and characteristically wrong with our cultural and political life. Even the recent lessening of militant protest or its sublimation in the conventional political process, following as it does so quickly upon the intense political and cultural conflicts of recent years, would seem to confirm this sentiment of rapid change. But the conflicts have not disappeared. We are still experiencing their impact in a muted but profoundly disquieting way.

Still with us is the feeling of disaffection from the high cultural tradition, which the counter culture has managed to identify with its principal enemy, bourgeois society. The feeling of disaffection is only the latest manifestation of what has been a characteristic cultural attitude in America, anti-intellectualism, though its usual source has been from the Right. If the "radical conscience" has not prevailed in cultural matters, neither have its adversaries. The counter culture has failed to achieve an alternative culture, and its hold on young people and guilt-ridden adults has waned. But the field has not been left to its unvanquished adversaries, as the continuing disaffection testifies.

And this is hardly surprising, given the bankruptcy of the custodians of the cultural tradition. Their failure to defend the tradition or to articulate a persuasive commitment to it is an unmistakable sign of bankruptcy. Humanistic study in America (and elsewhere) has long been vulnerable to criticism of a radical kind. Under the guises of "careful scholarship," "close reading," a modest concern with the "text itself," the elevation of "form" to the status of supreme value, literary study as carried on in the universities has too often trivialized the great texts to which it addressed itself. The formalistic attention to texts has contracted the idea of criticism to a conception of "scientific" competence—that is, the ingenuity and accuracy with which texts are read. What was in part a movement to disembarrass literary discussion of philistine attitudes toward literature—the reduction of literary activity to political propaganda, psychological therapy, and so forth—became a movement to obscure many of the real powers and vices of the literary imagination.

Here one would expect a radical criticism of literary study to find its occasion. But this has not occurred. And it will not occur so long as the radical idea is confined to an activist or therapeutic conception of academic work. Just as the New Criticism has contracted the critical idea to the idea of scientific competence (and in its preoccupation with form has evaporated the political content of literature), recent radical critics have contracted the critical idea to the testing of the political or therapeutic usefulness of literature: literature as an instrument of social change or self-fulfillment or communal experience. Genuine criticism (which is indispensable to the very idea of culture) cannot survive such subordination, because the very meaning and quality of the political life or self-fulfillment or communal experience (as well as specific ideals of politics, selfhood, and community) should be subject to imaginative and intellectual scrutiny.

High culture and criticism are, of course, not synonymous, despite Matthew Arnold's tendency to identify them a century ago. High culture has ideas, attitudes, ideological assumptions, which are themselves susceptible to criticism, even radical criticism. But any genuine criticism of high cul-

2

ture must proceed on the basis of an accurate sense of its strengths and weaknesses. The essay that follows is a critical attempt to disengage the idea of intellectual and literary culture from the distortions it has suffered from both sides. It has been provoked by occasions provided by the present cultural and political situation.

Relevance and the Authority of Culture

It is either ignorance or presumption to believe that
everything has been understood in any subject whatsoever
and that there is no longer any advantage to be derived
from the study and reading of the ancients.
D'Alembert, "Preliminary Discourse," in *The Encyclopedia*

"The breakdown of the university in the face of man's
present needs—the tremendous fact that the university has
ceased to be a *pouvoir spirituel* in Europe—is merely a consequence [of the fact that] the university is classicism."
Writing in 1932, Ortega y Gasset meant by classicism (he
might have said scholasticism) a pious antiquarian view of
the past. When culture is in the custody of those who me-
chanically bow to it, the tradition becomes spiritually power-
less. Against this spiritual poverty, Ortega made the radical
assertion: "I no longer believe in any ideas except the ideas
of shipwrecked men to answer certain peremptory questions
with reference to real life." Presumably some classics would
be responsive, others not. For Ortega high culture remains a
real possibility if not an unequivocal value.[1]

At least until recently, the university has not been a court
of shipwrecked men. I recall as an undergraduate in the
early fifties asking a philosophy professor what relevance
F. H. Bradley's post-Hegelian philosophy had to anything that
concerned my life. The implication of the question, as the
professor noted, was that the intellectual tradition had to be
validated by my interests and sensibility, regardless of their
present poverty. The rebuff was delivered sharply and precisely: it impressed me and everyone else in the class and

5

went unchallenged. Such a response is no longer possible. The student demand for relevance in humanistic study has grown more and more imperious. Moreover, it has received encouragement, even inspiration, from the most progressive teachers.

And for good reason. The humanities (history, literature, philosophy) have become increasingly vulnerable to challenge.* Humanists themselves can no longer say with assurance what the great books are; indeed, there is some question whether they are in possession of a subject, let alone a discipline. The vulnerability of the humanities is the culmination of a process that first becomes visible in the Enlightenment. The breakdown of the Christian synthesis in the seventeenth and the eighteenth centuries and the elevation of reason did not destroy the authority of Plato and Aristotle, for instance, but when they had been dislodged as the cornerstone of an intellectual and religious framework that had been taken for granted, it became possible to view their claims skeptically. Diderot makes precisely this argument in his essay in the *Encyclopedia*.

Today, when philosophy is advancing with gigantic strides, when it is bringing under its sway all the matters that are its proper concern, when its tone is the dominant one, and when we are beginning to shake off the yoke of authority and tradition in order to hold fast to the laws of reason, there is scarcely a single elementary or dogmatic book which satisfies us entirely. We find that these works are put together out of the productions of a few men and are not founded upon the truths of nature. We dare to raise doubts about the infallibility of Aristotle and Plato, and the time has come when the works that still enjoy the highest reputation will begin to lose some of their great prestige or

* It has been pointed out to me that in both the French and German traditions, from which humanities courses in America derive, *sciences de l'homme* and the *Geisteswissenschaften* include psychology, linguistics, and certainly the classics. I do not intend a restrictive definition of the humanities, but academic psychology (I exclude psychoanalysis) and linguistics have tended to operate on the models of the natural sciences—in which logic and mathematics play a prominent part. (This is also true of a good deal of academic philosophy—indeed, is perhaps its dominant tendency.)

even fall into complete oblivion. Certain literary forms—for want of the vital realities and actual custom that once served them as models—will no longer possess an unchanging or even a reasonable poetic meaning and will be abandoned; while others that remain, and whose intrinsic value sustains them will take on an entirely new meaning. Such are the consequences of the progress of reason, an advance that will overthrow so many old idols and perhaps restore to their pedestals some statues that have been cast down.[2]

In the nineteenth century the great books of western civilization (to use the modern phrase) had to find sanctions outside the orthodox dogmas. And yet the values of the Judeo-Christian and the classical traditions were sufficiently alive in the nineteenth century that it required relatively little adjustment to preserve the great books on secular grounds. Thus the gospels of Christ, no longer testifying to a supernatural reality, became an expression of the divine possibilities in the human soul. The differences between Augustine's and Ernest Renan's views of Christ, substantial as they are, do not overcome what they have in common, a belief in the centrality of Christ's life in western culture. The great books idea is an inheritance of the nineteenth century faith in the translatability of Christian and classical traditions to modern terms. Its "fathers" are the higher critics: Renan, David Friedrich Strauss, Matthew Arnold (of *Literature and Dogma* and *St. Paul and Protestantism*). For the present-day conscientious humanist it is no longer possible merely to assume this translatability. He is bound to be afflicted by a Nietzschean worry about the uses and abuses of history. How does the past count for the present? What is the authority for claiming this or that book as one of the great books? I do not mean that the lack of agreement is absolute, but it constitutes a strong tendency in our intellectual life.

This situation in the humanities has been exacerbated by a local cultural fact. The present generation of American students (or at least a significant portion of it) is unique in American history for its courageous militancy on political issues, notably civil rights and the war in Vietnam. Not all of the disaffected youth is political. An entire subculture of drug-oriented, militantly antipolitical hippies has evolved. And yet for all the opposition between the puritanical SDS and the mystical hippies,* they are united in their apocalyptic disaffection from the institutional life of the country. Together or separately, they vaunt their innocence against things as they are. Never before have students had so much moral authority for their teachers; never before have teachers had so little moral authority for their students. Not only have students come to feel their right to decide what they should be taught and how they should be taught, but that right has been assented to by their teachers.

Fifteen years ago such a situation would have been unthinkable. Whatever the motives for the silence of the fifties (the seduction of peacetime affluence or an inherited mistrust of Stalinist radicalism), the most sensitive of those who went to college in the forties and the fifties cannot help making an invidious comparison at their own expense between the present and the preceding generations. The present generation has become a conscience and a goad to the older generation. The upshot, educationally speaking, is a remarkable paradox.

I have brusquely united the hippies and the SDS, the mystics and the militants, on the ground of their disaffection from the existing order. Even deeper than the disaffection is a shared Manichean sense of their own innocence. (An innocence, to be sure, short-lived. For if it is true that anyone over thirty is not to be trusted, only a willed self-arrestment in the state of adolescence could save a young man from inevitable damnation.) Why is this generation different from all other generations? Because it does not share the original sin of Adam. Living in an apocalyptic situation, it has experienced a genuine conversion to the interests of mankind.

---

* The distinction does not exactly correspond to what is actually the case. Political militants "make the drug scene," but they often find they must choose between the strenuous lucidities of political work and the ecstatic temptation of whatever they may be on.

Unlike the generations that have gone before, it will act generously, passionately, authentically for peace, for community. Coming from middle and upper-middle class homes, the members of this generation do not suffer the resentful psychology of the have-nots. With the authority of innocence, their demand for relevance seems only natural. The implicit paradigm for the mind behind the current demand for relevance is *tabula rasa,* purged even of the vestiges of Christian, Judaic, or classical traditions. It is a mind informed by instant politics, instant joys, instant miseries, instant relationships, a mind purified of encumbrances to immediate instinct gratification.

It has been argued that the effect of modern life generally has been not only to undermine particular cultural traditions but to subvert the very authority of culture itself. The Freudian idea that the whole cultural life of man is a complex sublimation of primitive appetitive energies may not imply that the cultural life is disposable superstructure (for the probability is that much sublimation is at once necessary and irreversible), but the Freudian idea has contributed to a subversive, reductive atmosphere in which such an inference is drawn. "History is a nightmare from which I am trying to awake." Much of the radical gesturing toward curricular reform is really an illusory wishfulness (like Stephen's in *Ulysses*) that we can escape history.

The *tabula rasa* is a presumption of innocence. It is not the result of genuine discovery, for instance, that the Christian and classical traditions are no longer part of us. The enactments of our personality and character are involuntary, often compulsive. We are not free to choose what we are or even what we will do. We cannot simply wish away traditions that we have grown to dislike. The very dislike may be conditioned by the fact that they still possess us, if we do not possess them. If Judeo-Christian and classical traditions are still alive in all of us (as I suspect they are), despite attempts to deny them, then an education that fails to address itself to these traditions (I do not speak of arguing for or against them) would fail according to the ideal of relevance. The mere repudiation of these traditions does not have the effect of exorcism.

II

At the basis of every genuine intellectual act is the demand for relevance, but at critical moments in the history of culture the question of relevance may be part of the substance of the intellectual act. Such a moment is the European Renaissance and the *locus classicus* for the theme of relevance is the work of Montaigne. Again and again in his essays he speaks of a preoccupation with himself at the expense of a knowledge of other subjects. "I study myself more than any other subject. That is my metaphysics, that is my physics . . . In this universe of things I ignorantly and negligently let myself be guided by the general law of the world. I shall know it well enough when I feel it. My knowledge could not make it change its path; it will not modify itself for me." [3] There is even a trace of boasting in his claim that he is without real knowledge of anything except the self, a claim that would be philistine if it were not for his indisputable cultivation. The fact is of course that like a good Renaissance scholar (I use the word in its pristine not its modern specialized sense) Montaigne knows the classical writers very well. His work is filled with citations from Plutarch, Seneca, Ovid, and others.

Montaigne's problem was the problem of the Renaissance. It had come into a double inheritance, that of medieval Christianity and of classical antiquity, and it experienced the burden of culture as excessive. The Renaissance found its freedom in the eager embrace of classical learning and its repudiation of or indifference to the oppressive intellectual authority of one thousand years of Christian doctrine. In Montaigne's case the motive was not a particular religious or, for that matter, secular doctrine, but what Montaigne called his metaphysics and his physics: knowledge of the self.* Montaigne never challenges Church doctrine: he implicitly denies its reality for him. "We have no communication with being, because every human nature is always midway between birth and death, offering only a dim semblance and shadow of itself, and an uncertain and feeble opinion." [4]

The attraction that the classical writers had for Montaigne was in the secular and ethical content of their writings. They spoke directly to the question of how one lives in the world of Becoming, the only world that Montaigne knew. But we have not begun to understand the force of Montaigne's insistence that he knows only himself if we fail to realize that his relation to the classical writings was not at all scholarly in the sense in which we now mean the word. The passages from Plutarch and others are hardly quotations. They are all deeply lodged in his memory, part of the very lifeblood of his thought. (The frequent misrememberings confirm this.) If we read the essays properly we should not experience any difference between the text and the quotations. Everything is Montaigne.

Diderot's regret that Montaigne's pyrrhonism kept him from pursuing empirical knowledge reveals a misunderstanding of the strategy of the skepticism, for the skepticism is not the ultimate principle in Montaigne. Indeed, it was the skepticism that enabled him to become one of the great empiricists of the self. Its animus is not so much anti intellectual as anti-dogmatic. Dogmatism, as Montaigne knew, prevents one from knowing oneself, substitutes formula for

---

* I know that a formidable case has been made for Montaigne's fideism, but it seems to me that the case is made from the letter and not the spirit of Montaigne's work. Pascal, I think, was right to see Montaigne's pursuit of self as the anti-type to the Christian pursuit of God. Montaigne's humility about himself, his capacity to doubt his own powers, should not divert us from the fact of the pride of his enterprise—from the Christian point of view. His friend Estienne Pasquiar was unquestionably right: "While he gives the appearance of disdaining himself, I never read an author who esteemed himself as much as he." (Donald Frame, *Montaigne*, p. 311.)

perception. What he perceives and judges is not false but changeful, so that he must find a way (the way of the *essai*) to track the changefulness of life. When he claims to have no communication with Being, he is not asserting that reality or even truth is inaccessible to him. He would be making this assertion if he were committed to the platonic distinction between Being and Becoming, in which Becoming was seen as an illusive emanation of Being. Rather he uses platonic language and distinction in making an altogether different point: that the field of ethical speculation is Becoming. He is not interested in entering a theological controversy about the nature of Being (assuming there is such a thing). It is André Gide, one of Montaigne's most astute admirers, who perceives the strategic character of the skepticism when he characterizes Montaigne as having met Pilate's "atrocious question with a purely human version of Christ's answer: '*I* am the truth.' " [5]

What protects Montaigne's claim and performance from the charge of philistinism is that he is, despite his confessions of ignorance, a man of immense culture, so that the self, the touchstone for judging culture, has within its very marrow, so to speak, the cultural tradition, or at least a valuable portion of it. The contemporary American demand for relevance in its radical form does not presuppose the value of the cultural life. The touchstone for relevance is the naked unaccommodated self, and the result too often is a mutual impoverishment of self and culture.

The distinction I make between the current demand for relevance and Montaigne's exercise in relevance is not intended to be invidious in an elitist way, for I do not mean culture as aristocratic decoration or as a means of social climbing. By culture I mean an inward condition that enabled Montaigne to achieve an admirable self-knowledge and self-possession even in the light of his awareness of what was contemptible in human life and vain in human desire—to achieve this despite the convulsive times in which he lived. His culture was a kind of security against nihilism, for which of course he can claim no exclusive credit, for it was as much an achievement of his time as a personal triumph. Indeed, it is the contemporary loss of faith in culture that would make a contemporary Montaigne-like performance seem either an exercise in complacency or simply ridiculous. Montaigne's performance assumes a generally shared belief in the cultural life.

The decisive importance of the historical situation in making one belief or another possible can be illustrated by comparing Augustine with Montaigne. Appearing near the end of classical antiquity, Augustine too was the heir of the classical tradition, but as he shows in the famous episode of Alypius at the gladiatorial contest (in *The Confessions*), something had come into the life of Rome that rendered the classical tradition ineffectual.

Alypius, detesting the violence and brutality of gladiatorial spectacles, is nevertheless induced by friends to go to the amphitheater. Against his will, he is stirred by the cry of the audience and "he fell more miserably than he on whose fall that mightly clamor was raised . . . For directly he saw that blood, he therewith imbibed a sort of savageness; *nor* did he turn away, but fixed his eye, drinking in madness unconsciously, and was delighted with the guilty contest, and drunken with the bloody pastime . . . And from all this didst Thou, with a most powerful and most merciful hand, pluck him, and taughtest him not to repose confidence in himself, but in Thee—but not until longer after." [6]

In his masterful reading of this passage in *Mimesis,* Eric Auerbach sees the drama of Alypius as symbolic of the moral incapacity of enlightened classical culture with its emphasis on individualistic, aristocratic, moderate and rational self-discipline to cope with demonic experience. Alypius "trusts in his closed eyes and his determined will. But his proud individualistic self-reliance is overwhelmed in no time." A whole society may become so barbarously violent and so fascinated in its violence that the classical virtues, based on a partial psychology of the passions, become ineffective. Having lost their reality, the virtues become pious and platitudinous. The relevance ·of Christianity at such a moment is, as Auerbach remarks, that in "the fight against magical intoxication, it commands other weapons than those of the rational and individualistic ideal of antique culture; it is, after all, itself a movement from the depths, from the depths of the multitude as from the depths of immediate emotion; it can fight the enemy with his own weapons. Its magic is no less a magic than is bloodlust, and it is stronger because it is a more ordered, a more human magic, filled with more hope." [7]

Yet one thousand years later Montaigne was able to reassert the classical values and thereby prove them to be abiding possibilities in human life. What makes them a possibility for Montaigne is that there has come into the society of Montaigne's time a new sense of physical and social vitality and of the possibility of personal and social control.

Our present situation is particularly unfortunate, for neither the classical nor the Christian alternative seems particularly relevant. In the light of world wars, concentration camps, brainwashing, and the prospect of nuclear devastation, the Stoic or Epicurean virtues seem futile and absurd. Nor do we have available to us a magical alternative for the good, like Christianity. Centuries of rationalism have corroded the faith in the supernatural possibility. Drugs (the pursuit of narcotically induced ecstatic states) or anarchistic politics perhaps represent a kind of despairing hope in the possibility of such a magical alternative.

To chastise the present philistinism or vulgarity (the words themselves now have an embarrassing ring) would seem to be an exercise in futility. In the name of what can one argue for "cultural values"? What does it mean to be mature or cultivated or educated or self-possessed in a world of radical corruption and violence? The challenge, to be sure, is often put disingenuously, for it can be motivated by moral laziness.* But there is enough truth in the challenge to

* The demand for relevance is often no more than mere slogan. Its concrete implications are rarely considered. Is relevance a matter

14

make a convincing answer very difficult. And it is hard to imagine an answer that would not be nostalgic and elegiac.

One value of recalling moments in the past when the question of relevance was paramount is that we are reminded of how provisional all adjustments between culture and self are. The magical assurance that Alypius found in Christianity is no longer ours; the cheerful faith in the harmonies of the shifting equilibria of the self that sustained Montaigne's essays into the self seems merely complacent, and Diderot's triumphant assertion of the new authority of Reason impresses us as essentially optimistic. Should we find a new answer to the question, it would not serve forever.

However, the search for the answer need not be conducted, as it is now, in a mood of apocalyptic finality—as if only a complete and permanent answer will satisfy and prevent nihilism. It is well to remember that in *The Confessions* Augustine dramatizes the new authority of Christianity through the forms of classical rhetoric. Like Alypius he is a creature of classical culture, which he explodes without ever really abandoning it. To keep the traditional culture alive in us is not necessarily to affirm or celebrate it. Nor is it necessarily an act of pious pedantry. If the tradition contains within itself permanent human possibilities, then it is necessary to keep it alive as a kind of repository of options. Indeed, it may be especially necessary to do so at a moment when men feel secure in nothing, for they may be able to keep the life possibility going simply by worrying about the reality of lives lived in the past. But to keep the tradition as a repository of options requires that one achieve a historical

of confirming the student's sense of reality or of challenging it? If all the student requires is to be confirmed in his sense of things then it is hard to see the necessity of an education. Students, of course, continually surprise themselves by discovering how interesting and relevant a classic is and how dull a contemporary work may be. By being forced to read certain books students may discover what is relevant in the most unexpected places: classical Greece, that vast territory called the Middle Ages, Renaissance literature, the eighteenth century, and so on. The real student will never want to impoverish himself by excluding what is not fashionable, simply because it is unfashionable.

perspective on the present apocalyptic mood. One cannot at the same time believe that western civilization is at a final end and expect to manage even the minimal interest in the past that would make it a repository of options. Any attention to the past should teach one that apocalyptic moments are illusive in the sense of total cataclysmic change that would forever destroy past and present—barring total physical annihilation, which is always a possibility.

The rejection of the western tradition is of course in part a political act. Bad conscience about western culture, which is sometimes accompanied by hospitality to, if not pursuit of, eastern modes of consciousness, represents a recoil from western imperialism. If eastern consciousness relieves the troubled western soul from the anxieties of western society, part of the relief comes from the assuaging of conscience in the identification one makes with the culture of the oppressed against the culture of the oppressor—much like the recent insistence on the values of illiteracy.

How guilty western culture itself is in the role it plays in the arsenal of imperialism is a hard question to answer. Arthur de Gobineau and Rudyard Kipling are part of the western cultural tradition—and one can find assumptions of western superiority in many expressions of the western cultural tradition. Culture has learned only recently to accept the relativity of its authority. Like religion, every culture tends to assume universality for itself, a tendency that must be combatted—and the university is, or should be, particularly equipped to combat it. There is also the political use of culture which deforms its true character and for which it can hardly be held responsible. The use to which the Nazis put Plato and Nietzsche or to which the teachings of Christ have been put in colonial countries should not discredit Plato or Nietzsche or Christ.

Whatever the guilt of western culture may be, the fact remains that one cannot decide arbitrarily to live outside of it, just as one cannot decide to live outside one's body. Any deliberate exchange of culture is bound to be factitious, for a particular culture in the large anthropological sense (out of which high culture itself develops) is part of the soil of one's being. This does not mean that one is not free to appropriate alien cultural forms into one's own cultural system, an appropriation that doubtless alters the system in some way. But to try to exchange the system (which is what is involved in an apocalyptic rejection of western culture) is as futile as Picasso's attempting to become an Oriental or African artist, for all his facility with eastern and African forms.

III

When Jacob Burkhardt characterized culture as "a wavering authority" in *Force and Freedom,* he wrote out of a nineteenth century nostalgia for order and authority. Burkhardt was among the unhappy few of his century who expected the eventual triumph of nihilism. Culture, the only bastion of authority for the civilized man, was itself allied to the antidogmatic spirit of freedom which encourages nihilism, so it could hardly be expected to show the firmness of other forms of authority. Burkhardt in effect anticipated not only the radical challenge to culture in America, but the vulnerability of culture to the challenge. The imperatives of culture were ideally not coercive, and without coercion or the threat of coercion, authority has enormous difficulty sustaining itself. The demand for relevance is in effect an absolute refusal to be coerced; indeed the man who demands relevance often wants to dictate terms.

One of the more notable efforts to deal with the peculiarly vulnerable authority of culture is John Stuart Mill's *Utilitarianism,* a work that has received, it seems to me, the wrong kind of attention. Mill was writing at a time when the whole cultural tradition was being brought into question. The authority of religious and literary culture was challenged by men of scientific and utilitarian disposition.* Mill's essay is

* See, for instance, the debate between Matthew Arnold and Thomas Huxley on the values of a literary education vs. a scientific education (Huxley, "Science and Culture," 1880; Arnold, "Literature and Science," 1882).

an instructive case because he was uniquely responsive both to the disinterested claim of culture and to the interested claim of utility, that is, of relevance. There is a confidence and self-possession in Mill's attempt at mediation between the rival claims that is old-fashioned. Mill's voice is the voice of reason, dealing with cultural issues as if the triumph of nihilism were not imminent. It is a voice that now we almost never hear in cultural criticism.

Even admirers of John Stuart Mill rarely abandon their defensive positions when they speak of his utilitarianism. It is a tacit, if not open, agreement between admirer and critic alike that the utilitarian doctrine is an unfortunate legacy of Mill's upbringing, a gesture of piety to his father and Bentham, perhaps a compensation for the rough handling they often received in his writings. Mill's classic defense of the doctrine is generally taken as an attempt to sophisticate its crudities (for example, the conversion of pleasure from a quantity to a quality) and as a sort of shotgun marriage of vulgar hedonism with the moral and cultural ideals of the western tradition.

Mill viewed his performance quite differently: the alleged vulgarity of utilitarianism, in his view, was in the minds of the critics themselves. There is no reason to doubt that Mill believed sincerely in the fundamental premises of utilitarianism. He was a man of extraordinary intellectual and moral courage, too devoted to the pursuit of truth ever to sacrifice it on the altar of filial piety. It is of course possible that his filial piety was stronger than he imagined it to be and that he was thus misled about the nature of his devotion to his father's doctrine. But he was a man of rare self-understanding, and the view of Mill as pious son places an enormous burden of proof on his critics.* If read without prejudice (and as Mill himself knew so well, the humanistic prejudices

---

* Mill may have been unduly subject to the influences of his father and then of Harriet Taylor (as F. A. Hayek and more recently Gertrude Himmelfarb have argued), but I do not see evidence of undue influence in the integrity of his arguments.

against the philosophy of utility are very strong) Mill's essay on utilitarianism supplies an original and powerful rationale for a humanistic culture. The marriage between culture and utility is neither violent nor arbitrary. Before Mill, Shelley in his grandiloquent defense of the imagination (in "A Defense of Poetry") had argued for the utility of poetry (culture in its quintessential manifestation) against a vulgar utilitarianism that identified utility with scientific progress.

We have more moral, political and historical wisdom, than we know how to reduce into practice; we have more scientific and economical knowledge than can be accommodated to the just distribution of the produce which it multiplies. The poetry in these systems of thought, is concealed by the accumulation of facts and calculating processes. There is no want of knowledge respecting what is wisest and best in morals, government, and political economy, or at least what is wiser and better than what men now practise and endure. But we let 'I dare not wait upon I would, like the poor cat in the adage' (from *Macbeth*, Act I, scene vii, ll. 44–45). We want the creative faculty to imagine that which we know; we want the generous impulse to act that which we imagine; we want the poetry of life: our calculations have outrun conception; we have eaten more than we can digest. The cultivation of those sciences which have enlarged the limits of the empire of man over the external world, has, for want of the poetical faculty, proportionally circumscribed those of the internal world; and man, having enslaved the elements, remains himself a slave. To what but a cultivation of the mechanical arts in a degree disproportioned to the presence of the creative faculty, which is the basis of all knowledge, is to be attributed the abuse of all invention for abridging and combining labour, to the exasperation of the inequality of mankind? From what other cause has it arisen that the discoveries which should have lightened, have added a weight to the curse imposed on Adam? Poetry, and the principle of Self of which money is the visible incarnation, are the God and Mammon of the world.[8]

Shelley, it is important to note, never resorted to the argument that poetry is its own justification—poetry, he made clear, is a generator of value. For all the differences in manner and method, Mill and Shelley are substantially in agreement on the utility of culture. Despite appearances against it, it is a marriage based on compatibility and a mutuality of interests.

The two fundamental premises of utilitarianism are its hedonism (the justification of anything, including culture, by its capacity to give pleasure, to make people happy) and its empiricism (the formation of a morality on the basis of observation of what people really want). The two premises are the psychological and epistemological expressions of a single commitment to human happiness in its highest and most extensive sense. Mill's defense of utilitarianism is really an attempt to show the capacity of the cultural tradition to contribute to human happiness.

Mill's famous education had of course assumed a connection between culture and happiness. The happy man, in the shared view of Bentham and James Mill, was the completely rational man, informed and powerfully analytical. Mill's mental crisis severed the connection. He came to see that the analytic habits cultivated by his father and Bentham weakened those feelings that are the basis for happiness. After the crisis Mill clearly could no longer assume the connection. If culture was a source of human happiness, it would have to be consciously demonstrated. And yet even after his crisis Mill was predisposed to see culture and happiness in an alliance. He was not prepared to pursue the possibility that culture as an activity of the mind either as speculation or analysis is inimical to the spontaneous, passional life. Mill saw his suffering as a symptom of the absence of the *"culture* of the feelings."* The use of the word culture in this connection suggests Mill's civilized conception of the feelings. He never really entertained the possibility of irreconcilable warfare between mind and passion, between culture and the unconscious. Unlike Bentham (who was able to equate push-pin and poetry), Mill never achieved the radical empiricism that denied the self-evident authority of culture.

This self-evident authority consisted precisely in the stimulations to feeling that he found in the works of imagination he had hitherto neglected. "What made Wordsworth's poems a medicine for my state of mind, was that they expressed, not mere outward beauty, but states of feeling, under the excitement of beauty. They seemed to be the very culture of the feelings, which I was in quest of. In them I seemed to draw from a course of inward joy, of sympathetic and imaginative pleasure, which could be shared in by all human beings; which had no connexion with the struggle or imperfection, but would be made richer by every improvement in the physical and social condition of mankind. From them I seemed to learn what would be the perennial sources of happiness, when all the greater evils of life shall have been removed." [9] Doubtless there are those who possess by instinct what Mill had to find in books, but this does not diminish the resources that the cultural tradition possesses, resources that in unexpected, unforeseen ways suddenly become available to the needs of mind and soul.

Mill expanded the content of utilitarian philosophy to include, in Matthew Arnold's terms, "the best that has been known and thought." The hedonistic philosophy Mill inherited underwent a transformation in his hands that made it possible for him to assert that Socrates argued "the theory of utilitarianism against the popular morality of the so-called sophist." [10] But if he transformed utilitarianism by giving it the validation of western culture, he also transformed the conception of culture by compelling it to respond to the desire for happiness, even pleasure. What Mill does is liberalize the conception of culture without denying its authority. Mill is in a sense forced to do this by the exigencies of utilitarian philosophy, but the philosophical "compulsion" is enforced by a personal experience in which the cultural tradition is called upon during a time of ordeal to console and sustain the spirit.

One concern of *Utilitarianism* is the possibility of making the moral and artistic heritage of man the interior possession of men. Virtue ideally is not a burden to be borne, but the free expression of personality. "Virtue, according to the utilitarian doctrine, is not naturally and originally part of the end, but it is capable of becoming so, and, in those who love it disinterestedly it has become so, and is desired and cherished, not as a means to happiness, but as part of their happiness." [11]

The assent to culture must be unconditionally free—the disciple of culture never surrenders his franchise to a representative or a majority. He lives ideally in an Athenian democracy, or better in a Venetian anarchy. He may have to overcome himself (to use Nietzsche's phrase) in order to desire virtue and beauty, but he acts reflexively upon himself —is responsible only to himself. It is precisely for this reason that he must be demanding upon himself: to expect culture to satisfy the self requires that the self be a worthy object to gratify. One is inevitably led into circularity. The self is willy-nilly fed by culture and must be validated by culture, as Mill implicitly argues in *Utilitarianism,* before it can legitimately insist on relevance and the proper uses of culture.*

What happens when a man does not want virtue? Mill would like to bring him to the desiring of virtue, for it would never do to force him. A man's character and intellect must be educated to desire the best that has been known and thought. The ought remains but is always sensitive to the freedom to accept and reject. Mill's conception of moral liberty corresponds to the character of culture itself: the tension between its imperatives and freedom. What is admirable in Mill's performance is the poise that he maintains in mediating culture and utility.

Matthew Arnold, the great nineteenth century apostle of

* In America the conceptions of self and culture are polarized. Not the least of the complex and many reasons for this is a powerful utilitarian psychology (in the narrow Benthamite sense) born of a triumphant industrialism. In a time when the cultural life is repressive, it is a source of strength for the self not to be defined by culture, so that it can judge and even reject the tradition. But in the American case there is the greater danger of a false and impoverishing dichotomy in which the useful demand demeans both self and culture.

culture, was a less successful mediator. If Mill discovers in culture the appropriate faith for the free man, Arnold dramatizes (perhaps overemphasizes) the imperatives of culture, its disciplining effect on the human spirit. A liberal himself, Arnold was nevertheless mistrustful of the powerful libertarian notions that formed a large part of the moral atmosphere of nineteenth century England. Arnold was understandably repelled by the unholy alliance between freedom and philistinism in the nineteenth century, which he satirizes to considerable effect in *Culture and Anarchy* in the chapter "Doing as One Likes." To do as one likes (from commercial and philistine motives) is to express one's ordinary self, not one's best self. For Arnold true freedom is not laissez-faire but intellectual, moral, and artistic power: it is the capacity to perfect oneself.

Arnold's mistrust of philistine libertarianism leads, however, to a serious misconception of the precarious poise that exists between cultural imperatives and freedom. The trouble arises in Arnold's instances. In *Culture and Anarchy* he invokes the authority of culture (the interests of the best self) in condemning Colonel Wilson's failure to repress with vigor the political riots of the "roughs" in Hyde Park. Arnold illicitly identifies culture with the state, that is, with law and order.[12] In his instances he is willing to confound the actual state (itself an expression of the ordinary self, that is, of egoistic business and political interests) with the ideal state. Moreover, Arnold's peremptory emotion about the "wrongdoing" of the roughs suggests a mind actuated by motives other than cultural motives. Even if the roughs were in the wrong, culture could not enlighten them by more vigorous police action: for culture can only work in the willing susceptibility of the mind to enlightenment. (Culture's address is to reason and consequently it must work through persuasion not force. Indeed, one of the limitations of culture from a radical or revolutionary point of view is that it is weak in activist impulse when activism is called for.) For all his professed liberalism, Arnold is willing to advocate vigorous police action in the name of culture because of a conservative need for law and order that transcends at least in this instance his championship of culture.*

IV

Notwithstanding the conservative side of Arnold's conception of culture, the idea in the nineteenth century had heretical force. Nietzsche conceived culture (in its vital form) as the incarnation of the subversive spirit of freedom in opposition to the state. Even in the England of Matthew Arnold and John Stuart Mill, culture was suspected by the common intelligence as incompatible with the ancient beliefs "if not simply equivalent to apostasy." [13] For Arnold culture is the best spirit of democracy. In our time, culture in one of its principal meanings has lost both its positive and its critical character. The anthropologists have extended the meaning of the word to cover mores, habits, the forms and patterns of human behavior in society; in such usage, culture becomes simply a definitional term and loses its partisan spiritual and political character. In the anthropological view, culture is a given.

In psychoanalytic thought culture has remained problematic and controversial. Freud saw culture (which for him embraced habits, forms and patterns of human behavior, as well as the arts and sciences) as sublimation: the ambiguous incarnation of both the reality and the pleasure principles. Culture may impose itself repressively on the libido; it may also provide avenues of expression for libidinous and emotional energies. Freud's vision of culture is governed by a

---

* Arnold's strictures against political protest go much beyond the matter of violence: he was adamantly opposed to nonviolent mass demonstrations as well. And his notion of dealing with rioters is antediluvian. He quotes his father with approval: "As for rioting, the old Roman way of dealing with *that* is always the right one; flog the rank and file, and fling the leaders from the Tarpeian Rock!" (*Culture and Anarchy*, ed. J. Dover Wilson, Cambridge at the University Press, 1957, p. 203.)

sense of its repressiveness (while acknowledging its other side), a repressiveness that he at once regrets and affirms as necessary to the formation of character and the survival of civilization.

The view of culture as repressive (without the significant qualifications of this view one finds in *Civilization and Its Discontents*) has become the leading motif, so to speak, of recent radical revisionists of psychoanalytic doctrine—like Herbert Marcuse, Norman O. Brown, and R. D. Laing. Under the auspices of psychoanalysis (or of a debased psychoanalysis) the historical ideal of culture as a vehicle of freedom, of the formation of character and mind, has come to be seen as essentially negative. That idea needed the qualifying vision of Freud, whose work dramatizes the price paid for the powers culture bestows. But to resolve the ambiguity of the Freudian perspective on culture to its negative element is simultaneously to distort the psychoanalytic idea and to arrive at an unwarranted nihilism.

When a contemporary radical claims that "all education involves an expensive exchange of instinctual life for symbolic life, an exchange which in the case of literary education is facilitated by an appeal to the senses," [14] he is using psychoanalytic language to distort the psychoanalytic idea for his own purpose. The young man or woman coming to literature in a serious way in the late teens does not give up instinctual freedom in exchange for symbols. The exchange had been made long ago and the currency involved in the transaction, as we learn from common psychoanalytic wisdom, occurs between instinctual life and parental authority and security. (The political parable of this exchange is Ivan's dream of the Grand Inquisitor in *The Brothers Karamazov*.) An education may enforce the case for parental and social authority, but it may also create in the susceptible student the sense of the possibility of instinctual freedom. That is, a literary education may involve the promise of regaining the instinctual freedom one is supposed to have lost in early childhood. And if one takes the psychoanalytic argument seriously, one must keep in mind the price of moral insecurity that one pays for instinctual freedom.

Moreover, the current radical view tends to confuse the valuable idea of freedom with the inchoate confusions often generated by the early exchange that occurs between parent and child. The same critic who laments the surrender of instinctual freedom in the educational process acknowledges the authority of his students who exhibit a resistance analogous (in his view) "to the skewed grammars of Dickinson, Hopkins, Rimbaud etc. . . . which does not achieve the legitimacy of art [a curiously conservative phrase], but which as a teacher I cannot override without denying the student's sense of his own truth." He goes on to say that "we have come to the point where dialectal illiterates, those who cannot learn, or have learned not to learn, or those who are mad are the only good students." [15] But the preliterate confusions of young people (as well as of older people) may be authentic without self-clarity. Nor do they necessarily reflect power over oneself or power to express oneself, which one expects from instinctual freedom. The difference between Dickinson, Hopkins, and Rimbaud on the one hand and the dialectal illiterates on the other, a difference that makes the former artists and the others not, is that the skewed grammar of the poets is an expression of energy that achieved form or the articulateness of beauty—which often presupposes conscious control. (There is in the "legitimacy of art" a mastery of the tension between orthodox and skewed grammar.) This is not to say that the skewed grammar of a gifted "illiterate" student cannot be rewarding, but the literary equivalent of much of the skewed grammar one hears spoken is Jack Kerouac, writing limited in its easy use of conjunctions, impoverished, and boringly repetitive.

The radical argument is a populist version of the cult of the artist, which developed in the nineteenth century under the auspices of romanticism. Instinctual freedom is the artist's dream: "eternity protruding into time" in Rilke's phrase; "beauté, volupté, calme, luxe" in Baudelaire's

26

phrase. It is the irrepressible vitalistic spirit of revolt. In the great romantics the dreams of freedom are accompanied by nightmares of terror. Rilke's terrible angels, Lawrence's demons, and Nietzsche's eternally recurrent world of destructive energy suggest the terror and even the impossibility of the dream and consequently the need to contain and express the dream. This tension is figured by Nietzsche in the gods Dionysus and Apollo. The populist version expands the franchise of the dream and suppresses the nightmares of terror, so that Dionysus can become a god with Apollonian wisdom—thereby making the appearance of Apollo unnecessary.

There is another deep confusion in the radical (counter cultural) argument. The confusion lies in the implicit identification of libidinal freedom with the passion for justice. "For the radical imagination there can be no unreal persons." * And we are told that education turns us off from the suffering of others.[16] This supposes that dialectal illiterates come to school with an instinctive understanding of the reality of others and an instinctive compassion for their suffering, which education either attenuates or destroys. But libidinal freedom, on any psychoanalytic understanding of human experience, has little to do with the sense of justice. Rousseau, it is true, found the sense of justice rooted in the instinct of compassion, which he intuited as natural to human beings. But even if compassion is an instinct, it is already attenuated and suppressed in the earliest psychic battles one wages, and compassion itself, let alone the more complex idea of justice that evolves from the instinct of compassion, must be relearned. Indeed, education may increase our awareness of the sufferings of others and of the remedies for alleviating them. The source of this misunderstanding of the relation of freedom to the educational process is in the guilt which the educated person feels about dialectal illiterates, and in his recently acquired unwillingness to win easy

* This is patently untrue. The adversary is often turned into a cipher or, worse, a monster, in Manichean fashion.

27

victories over them and consequently his need to give authority to illiteracy in order to suppress the authority of his literacy.

The present political situation has, in my view, given the students an authority beyond their capacities. The right to determine educational policy—that is, what should be taught, how it should be taught, and who shall teach—is not deducible from any of their actual achievements. In practice, of course, decisions are usually made by faculty; my criticism is directed toward an ever increasing compulsion among university teachers to give students what they want or at least what the teachers think they want. If humanists cannot decide among themselves what their subject is, it does not follow that students should do the deciding, for the cultivated and conscientious skepticism of men who have in some sense mastered the tradition obviously has superior authority to an ignorant and precipitous response to it.*

It is not a matter of turning a particular work into a sacred text or a particular writer into a god (for that way lies intellectual servility and pedantry): it is a matter of faith in discourse, in imagination, in the very medium of thought, which the current mood of apocalyptic repudiation makes so difficult, indeed for some impossible.

The relation between teacher and student is analogous to the relation between the work and the reader. The transaction called education can occur only through dialectic, that reciprocal generosity in which there is battle, resistance, submission, and still more battle. The alternatives are pedantry on the one hand, and philistinism on the other.

* This statement need not be construed as implying practical exclusion of students from the curriculum-making process. It is simply intended as a "conservative" caveat against ignorant presumptions that too often animate revolutionary enthusiasms. I would like to see attitudes affected, not suppressive rules imposed. I want serious, honest discussion, not administrative fiats.

Cultural Radicalism in America and England

When Ortega y Gasset, like Nietzsche before him, attacks the apostles of culture, the target is not the spiritual idea immanent in the cultural tradition, but rather certain conceptions of culture, which have come to seem identical with the idea of culture itself. Cultural philistinism is one such conception. The *bourgeois gentilhomme,* uneasy about his social status, has a passion to acquire the genteel airs of the aristocrat, for which the *via media* is the cultural life or rather the decorative aspect of the cultural life. It is hardly necessary to note its characteristics: an appetite for fashionable cultural artifacts, a pseudo-intellectual phrasemongering (pretentiousness), a consumer's relation to the arts without any attention to the art of consumption. Although the contemporary *bourgeois gentilhomme* in America would hardly think of himself as aspiring to the status of aristocrat, middlebrow culture (as defined in the fifties by cultural critics like Dwight MacDonald) is a somewhat more sophisticated version of the culture of Molière's hero.

There is still another conception of culture that is vulnerable to the kind of criticism we find in Ortega and Nietzsche: the pedantry of the academic tradition.* On the analogy of

---

* I am not sure that the "highbrow" does not also participate in the game of cultural philistinism to the extent that he develops an obsessive interest in distinguishing the various positions of the brow. This kind of highbrow activity easily turns into self-congratulation, which marks the cultural philistine. The obsession with high, middle, and low cult in the fifties fueled a snobbery that masked itself as intellectualism. The characteristic work of highbrow criticism was the hatchet job on the middlebrow performance (for example, MacDon-

the religious tradition (an analogy by no means fortuitous) culture is a canon of "great books," touchstones as Arnold called them, by which we live or should live. The analogy is not fortuitous because the apostles of culture, men like Arnold and Renan, who simultaneously desacralized religious culture and raised secular culture to a quasi-religious status, had preserved a theological habit of mind, even as they lost their faith in a supernatural being.* In its inception the cultural idea, even in its canonical form, had a certain vitality, if only because the makers or remakers of the tradition are forced to say why one or another book is part or not part of the cultural tradition. Whatever one thinks of the particulars of Arnold's judgment of Chaucer, the very act of reading Chaucer out of the canon of touchstones is an act of personal intellectual vitality. Arnold is measuring his man against his sense of life. But once the canon is produced, a kind of intellectual dependence in the professors of the canon is created which makes extremely difficult the free disinterested intellectual act. The professor is generally the commentator, the writer of marginal notes to texts already declared to be worthy. Occasionally an unusual professor (like F. R. Leavis— though, significantly, he was kept from his professorship an unconscionably long time) will try to remake the canon, which of course is an attempt to remake the cultural life. More than the "mere" valuing of books is involved. It is canonical culture to which Ortega and Nietzsche oppose real life.

---

ald on Cozzens or Fiedler on the Rosenberg letters). At the moment that one engages serious art, self-consciousness about highbrowism must disappear. (See Harold Rosenberg, "Pop Culture, Kitsch Criticism" in *The Tradition of the New,* New York: McGraw Hill, 1965.)

   * The cultural canon does not have the fixity of the Scriptures, because it is explicitly a human creation, susceptible to the vagaries of human fortune and history. The religious idea of the canon is only an analogue to the literary tradition with all the limitations of an analogue. T. S. Eliot's view in "Tradition and the Individual Talent" that every new book remakes the tradition is still persuasive. Of course, if one can no longer subscribe to the idea of a tradition, one is simply responding to discrete literary phenomena.

But life for both of them is not merely daily living: it is the sense of life contained within great cultural achievements. Philistinism is insensitive to the intellectual energy, the spiritual aspiration, the complexity and beauty of the cultural act. Nietzsche's and Ortega's attacks on culture should not be confused with the philistine's resentment toward culture, when he is not affecting it.

What has been distressing about the current cultural radicalism in America is that it has joined up without knowing it with the dominant philistine resentment toward intellectual and artistic culture. Though the exponents of the counter culture enjoy the prestige of being radical, they show little interest in the life of the mind in its radical aspect.* If one does not identify the idea of radicalism with a particular political or cultural partisanship (which is now the habit as it was the habit of the thirties) then a "reactionary elitist" like Nietzsche or a "liberal elitist" like Ortega might be regarded as the most interesting kind of radical—that is, one who subversively goes to the roots of all partisanships. (Contemporary radicals are for the most part insensitive to the tension that always exists between political activism and intellectual radicalism.) "To the extent that a society is suspicious of a learned or professional clergy, so far will it be disposed to repudiate or deprive its intellectual class, whether religious or secular. In modern culture the evangelical movement has been the most powerful carrier of this kind of religious anti-intellectualism, and of its antinomian

* Not all radicals endorse the argument for a counter culture. Many would repudiate the ambivalence, indifference, or even hostility that the counter culture exhibits to politics—as I shall show. Moreover, those of Marxist persuasion would prefer to oppose "working class" culture to "bourgeois" high culture. However disaffected middle class youth may be from the prevailing cultural values, any culture that it generates out of its own experience is bound to have a bourgeois character, from a Marxist point of view. The difficulty for the Marxists, of course, is that the working class has been so bourgeoisified that they must look far and wide for a working class culture that can be called radical with any authority. This is one reason why the counter culture has had authority among radicals.

impulse. Of course, America is not the only society whose culture has been affected by evangelicalism. But in America, religious culture has been largely shaped by the evangelical spirit, for here the balance of power between evangelicalism and formal religion was long ago overwhelmingly tipped in the direction of the former. To see how much this was true one need only compare the historical development of religion in Britain, where the Establishment was prepared to absorb and domesticate a large part of the evangelical movement, with that of America, where the evangelicals rapidly subverted, outstripped or overwhelmed the older liturgical churches." [1] The suspicion of the learned or professional clergy, the antinomian feeling that one's personal living sense of the truth is superior to the operations of the intellect: these are powerful themes in the counter culture, and they are often presented in the evangelical style.*

In *The Making of the Counter Culture,* the most articulate manifestation of the counter culture, Theodore Roszak celebrates a culture based on what he calls visionary experience, but what comes through his account of visionary experience is a sentimental call for love and experience and an unearned hostility to science, which is variously identified with "research," "fact and theory mongering," "heaps of knowledge," "technology." Indeed, Roszak's hostility extends to the whole intellectual enterprise. His rhetoric and feeling are at once mystical and philistine: that peculiarly evangelical combination, American style. "To ask [the] question [of what constitutes true knowledge] is to insist that the primary purpose of human existence is not to devise ways of piling up ever greater heaps of knowledge, but to discover ways to live from day to day that integrate the whole of our nature by way of yielding nobility of conduct, honest fellowship,

---

* Woodstock Nation was less extraordinary than it seemed. America has witnessed evangelical revivals before. To be sure, the leftist aura of Woodstock made it unique, but its ultimate interest in music rather than words—that is meaning as a form of communication—made it clear that its primary significance was religious experience, states of feeling rather than political education and action.

and joy. And to achieve those ends, a man need perhaps 'know' very little in the conventional, intellectual sense of the word. But what he does know and may only be able to express by eloquent silence, by the grace of his most commonplace daily gestures, will approach more closely to whatever reality is than the most dogged and disciplined intellectual endeavor. For if that elusive concept 'reality' has any meaning, it must be that toward which the entire human being reaches out for satisfaction, and not simply some fact-and-theory mongering fraction of the personality. What is important, therefore, is that our lives should be as *big* as possible, capable of embracing the vastness of those experiences which, though yielding no articulate, demonstrable propositions, nevertheless awake in us a sense of the world's majesty." [2] The sentimentality of the passage is beyond comment. Roszak would cry foul if his adversary rendered the counter culture idea in the way he renders the intellectual enterprise, by identifying it with its worst instances, for example if his adversary identified spiritual exaltation with drug addiction or the moral sentiments with Puritan punitiveness.

For Roszak science is in essence corrupt. It is false consciousness in its cult of objectivity. In Roszak's view, science is the subjective manipulation of experience to serve inhuman aims. Science devitalizes experience and dehumanizes the scientist.

Whatever the scientific method may or may not be, people think they are behaving scientifically whenever they create an In-Here within themselves which undertakes to know without an investment of the person in the act of knowing. The necessary effect of distancing, of estranging In-Here from Out-There may be achieved in any number of ways: by the intervention of various mechanical gadgets between observer and observed; by the elaboration of chilly jargons and technical terms that replace sensuous speech; by the invention of strange methodologies which reach out to the subject matter like a pair of mechanical hands; by the subordination of the particular and immediate experience to a statistical generalization; by appeal to a professional standard which excuses the observer from responsibility to anything other than a lofty abstraction—such as "the pursuit of truth," "pure research," etc. All these protective strategies are especially compatible with natures that are beset by timidity and fearfulness; but also with those that are characterized by plain insensitivity and whose habitual mode of contact with the world is a cool curiosity untouched by love, tenderness, or passionate wonder. Behind both such timidity and insensitivity there can easily lurk the spitefulness of a personality which feels distressingly remote from the rewards of warm engagement with life. It is revealing that whenever a scientific method of study is brought into play, we are supposed to regard it as irrelevant, if not downright unfair, to probe the many very different motivations that may underlie a man's desire to be purely objective. It is little wonder, then, that the ideal of objectivity can be easily invoked to cover a curiosity of callousness and hostility, as well as a curiosity of affectionate concern. In any event, when I convince myself that I can create a place within me that has been cleansed of all those murky passions, hostilities, joys, fears, and lusts which define my person, a place that is "Not-I" and when I believe that it is *only* from the vantage point of this Not-I that reality can be accurately perceived, then I have begun to honor the myth of objective consciousness.[3]

But, as we know, timid and insensitive people can protect themselves behind high-sounding moral and sentimental generalizations. Scientists may be motivated by a passion for truth or by the spirit of invention and ingenuity. Poets may be motivated by the desire for publication. Scientists may be cool and detached in the laboratory and warm and tender at home. Poets may be passionate in their verse and despicable in their personal relationships. The converse of all these statements may also be true. Roszak's "sociology" of science is the most banal nineteenth century romanticism (note I am not characterizing romanticism in its essence). Moreover, the cult of objectivity does not characterize all scientific philosophy. One may find it in empiricism, behaviorism being its latest manifestation. It does not characterize a Cartesian rationalist like Noam Chomsky, whose commitments to science and social justice are passionate and (on his own account) related.

Roszak believes that he finds support for his view that science is elitist and arbitrary in Thomas Kuhn's *The Structure of Scientific Revolutions*. But Roszak takes a feature of one view of scientific activity and distorts it. "Thomas Kuhn, who has looked at the matter more carefully, has recently thrown strong and significant doubt on this 'incremental' conception of the history of science. His contention comes close to suggesting that the progressive accumulation of 'truth' in the scientific community is something of an illusion, created by the fact that each generation of scientists rewrites its textbooks in such a way as to select from the past what is still considered valid and to suppress the multitude of errors and false starts that are also part of the history of science. As for the all-important principles of validation that control this natural selection of scientific truth from era to era—the so-called 'scientific method'—Kuhn is left unconvinced that they are quite as purely 'rational' or 'empirical' as scientists like to think." [4] Kuhn, to be sure, is concerned to show how uncritical attitudes toward assumptions that scientists make about reality can be fostered in such a situation. But he never suggests that the assumptions are simply arbitrary or that the rules of the game are contrivances with no relation to truth, contrivances that foster the mystique of the scientific elite, as Roszak does. It is a gross travesty of Kuhn's book to suggest that it supports the view that scientific knowledge is a pure exercise in bad faith, that its difficulty is not a function of the complexity of the subject, but of the desire of those who propagate the difficulty to maintain their elitist privileges. "The very existence of science depends upon vesting the power to choose between paradigms in the members of a special kind of community. Just how special that community must be if science is to survive and grow may be indicated by the very tenuousness of humanity's hold on the scientific enterprise . . . . The group that shares [the solutions to problems] may not, however, be drawn at random from society as a whole, but its rather well-defined community of the scientist's professional compeers. One of the strongest, if still unwritten, rules of scientific life is the prohibition of appeals to heads of state or to the populace." [5] By showing that there is a subjective element in the sciences and exposing the myth of objectivism, Kuhn does not discredit science—on the contrary, he tries to give a truer philosophical estimate of the powers and limitations of science than the objectivist account yields.

Roszak admits that "the present situation makes it next to impossible for many of us who teach to carry on much in the way of education among the dissenting youth, given the fact that our conventional curriculum, even at its best, is grounded in the dominant Western tradition," whose vast resources he illicitly identifies with "three hundred years of scientific and technical work in the West." [6] This despite the fact that Christianity, Jakob Boehme, and Wordsworth (which Roszak invokes as allies of the counter culture) have formed and been formed by the western tradition. (Though the animus of Roszak's book is directed chiefly against science, its profound anti-intellectualism extends to the humanities as well.)

At times Roszak shows some anxiety about the nihilistic thrust of the counter culture. For instance, he is concerned with the insufficient reflectiveness of the young about the possibility that "the pursuit of Dionysian frenzy and the exploration of the non-intellective power will . . . degenerate into maniacal nihilism." [7] But he shows his affinity with the nihilistic tendency when he characterizes the appropriate relation of the student to knowledge as involving the realization that "knowledge [note, not pseudo-knowledge] is there not for the asking, but for the debunking." [8] (Perhaps Roszak meant demystifying, even so the slip, if it is that, reveals the crudity of his "intellectual" radicalism.) *

* It is true that the way science is usually taught in the universities justifies radical criticism, for teachers of science rarely give the

Against the "irrelevance" of the western tradition, Roszak proposes a cultural idea, which he admits is minimal and the expression of which he sometimes finds "difficult to take." "Much of what is most valuable in the counter culture does not find its way into literate expression—a fact well worth bearing in mind if one wants to achieve any decent understanding especially of what the more hip-bohemian young are up to. One is apt to find out more about their way by paying attention to posters, buttons, fashions of dress and dance—and especially to the pop music, which now knits together the whole thirteen to thirty age group. Timothy Leary is probably correct in identifying the pop and rock groups as the real 'prophets' of the rising generation. Unfortunately, I find this music difficult to take, though I recognize that one probably hears the most vivid and timely expression not only in the lyrics of the songs but in the whole raucous style of their sound and performance. While one cannot avoid being impressed with the innovation and dazzling sophistication of the best pop music, I fear I tend to find much of it too brutally loud and/or too electronically gimmicked up. I am not particularly in favor of turning musicianship and the human voice into the raw material of acoustical engineering. I also feel that the pop music scene lends itself to a great deal of commercial sensationalizing: the heated search for startling new tricks and shocks." [9] This rather extraordinary admission is conveniently tucked away in the bibliographical notes. The counter culture has too been seduced by technology, the great cultural achievement of America. Though "electronically gimmicked up" singing is a relatively harmless instance of technology, it is significantly symptomatic that the counter culture, which programmatically declared itself an enemy of technocracy, should in its main "prophetic" expression prove so unresisting to the temptations of technology.

---

student an insight into the curiosity, the intellectual passions that animate the scientific enterprise. The current critique of university teaching may be producing beneficent changes in this respect.

The philistinism of Roszak's position is a watered-down version of anti-intellectualist arguments, some of them made by men of genius and intellectual power. Dostoevsky, Nietzsche, Kierkegaard, and Lev Shestov (to name only a few) have in one way or other protested—in behalf of personality, freedom, imagination—against the constraining power of reason, the worship of scientific necessity. The critical difference between these men and Roszak (who is symbolic for me of the new anti-intellectualism) is that not only were they in possession of a rich intellectual culture, but they used against culture intellectual weapons derived from it, and they fully appreciated the price they were paying in divesting themselves of it. One cannot find in the great anti-intellectualists a facile dismissal of "heaps of knowledge." The hatred of reason was for them a hatred of a demonic power. "The laws of reason and morality," Shestov tells us, "were deeply imbedded in [Nietzsche]. They had somehow become part of his spiritual being; to tear them out without killing his soul seemed to him as impossible as to extract the skeleton of a man without killing the man. In his view, just as in ours, these laws express our deepest nature; beyond good and evil, beyond the truth, there is only the void, nothingness where everything appears. Nevertheless, it is there that one can, one must seek omnipotence, the power that will save man from death." [10]

The significance of Roszak's book, it seems to me, is that it is a characteristic product of American anti-intellectualism, which we have had and probably always will have with us. Though Roszak's argument has academic origins and dresses itself in intellectual garb, it shows none of the dialectical pain of renunciation that we find in the works of the great European anti-intellectualists who were trying to rid themselves of a possession. If the counter culture is already moribund (cultural and political attitudes show a high rate of mortality these days), the profound American hostility to intellect is not dead. I suspect that the negative influence of the counter culture will persist in the feeling it has generated against the cultural tradition. Indeed, this feeling has become the stock-in-trade of commencement speakers and university administrators, whose own cultural philistinism provides them with an easy rhetoric for evading a real confrontation with the intellectual and moral challenges of the cultural tradition.

The reason for the rather facile rejection of intellectual culture in America is that it never really took hold here, except in certain places, among certain groups, and at certain times.* It never became in Richard Hoggart's phrase a "lived-in virtue." High culture has in fact been the long suffering counter culture in America. Among the casualties of the conflict between the "two cultures" have been the expatriates Henry James, T. S. Eliot, and Ezra Pound and the internal emigrés Hawthorne and Melville. In the current feeling that high culture is irrelevant, we have an unwitting expression of the triumph of the dominant culture. It is ironic that the functional or utilitarian conception of culture should once again assert itself through those who are militantly opposed (at the conscious level) to a society that tends to see its members as productive or consuming functions. It is no accident that what calls itself the counter culture now has such close affinity with the dominant commercial culture in its music, its literature, its style, its appetites. Whatever may be the intrinsic merit of the Beatles or hard rock their

* For instance, "it is doubtful," as Richard Hofstadter reminds us, "that any community ever had more faith in the value of learning and intellect than Massachusetts Bay." And Hofstadter cites Moses Coit Tyler: "Only six years after John Winthrop's arrival in Salem harbor, the people of Massachusetts took from their treasury the fund from which to found a university; so that while the tree-stumps were as yet scarcely weather browned in their earliest harvest fields, and before the nightly howl of the wolf had ceased from the outskirts of their villages, they had made arrangements by which even in that wilderness their young men could at once enter upon the study of Aristotle and Thucydides, or Horace and Tacitus, and the Hebrew Bible . . . The learned class was indeed an order of nobility among them." In his history, Hofstadter traces the decline or abandonment of the intellectualist ideal. *Anti-Intellectualism in American Life* (New York: Alfred Knopf, 1952), pp. 59–60.

double success in the main culture and the counter culture puts in serious question the resistant qualities of the counter culture.

There are of course themes in the counter culture that are not philistine in origin (indeed, are even anti-philistine), though so often, as in many of Roszak's formulations, they have a philistine cast. For instance, the ambivalence toward politics in the counter culture (even toward radical politics) is the result of a genuine perception of the political will, whatever its intentions to maintain, sometimes worsen, the repressive character of the system. Roszak speaks [11] of "the futility of a politics which concentrates itself single-mindedly on the overthrowing of governments, or ruling classes, or economic systems. This brand of politics finishes with merely redesigning the turrets and the towers of the technocratic citadel. It is the foundations that must be sought. And those foundations lie among the ruins of the visionary imagination and the sense of community." * The counter culture speaks in the name of vision and community.

There is, to be sure, an element in the political life that is congenial to the counter culture: the pleasure and fear in

---

* The term "cultural revolution" has been used to cover a world-wide movement (of feeling as well as action) of youth, though the phrase probably originates in China where the most momentous "cultural revolution" has occurred. Mao, like Roszak, understands the pitfalls of "merely redesigning the turrets and towers" of social life, though he would doubtless recoil from the anarchistic poeticizing about the work of the "visionary imagination." To make the revolution one must spiritually revolutionize the revolutionaries: in America before the revolution, in China after the revolution. But the differences between East and West (particularly in its American version) are significant. The anarchistic poeticizing of the American counter culture with its exuberant life style, its traffic with drugs, its open courting of ecstatic states of feeling, is essentially different from the puritan asceticism of the Red Guard, for whom moral purity rather than spiritual and sensual exaltation is the principal value. Both the counter culture and the Red Guard are hostile to bourgeois acquisitiveness, but in the easy and luxurious style of the counter culture one senses the legacy of the material riches that capitalist culture has produced (which is one reason for working class suspicion of the radical young in America).

spontaneous resistance in the streets, in the mounting of mass demonstrations. But organizing committees and groups, holding long meetings, learning to use whatever power one gains—all this can hardly be subsumed under the word joy. And yet according to Daniel and Gabriel Cohn-Bendit, "Revolution must be born of joy and not of sacrifice." [12] The counter culture suffers from an unresolved conflict between wanting its paradise now and fighting for it.

It is to the credit of the American counter culture that it has perceived however dimly that an ambiguous conception of culture that is effectively puritanical and utilitarian and ideally hedonistic and Dionysian is finally insupportable. But the exponents of the counter culture have resolved the conflict in a most unsatisfactory way. They have opted for a minimal conception of culture in which the active element is banished. If the counter culture creates problems for political activity, the problems for intellectual work are graver still. For the style of the counter culture (its defiant visibility in the streets, for instance) has at least immediate political impact, whereas the constraints and discipline of intellectual work suggest all the misery of psychic repression that the joyful counter cultural style is supposed to overcome.

The energies of intellect and art, having been identified with the repressive puritanical conception of culture, have been exorcised by the new culture. Without the necessary cultivation the wise passiveness of the counter culture is particularly vulnerable to the sense of emptiness and ennui that always threatens in modern life. Having rid itself of the anxieties of ambition, it is now threatened by the anxieties of emptiness. And that emptiness tends to be filled by the artifacts of the dominant commercial culture. Not that the pursuit of high culture or art can provide guarantees against ennui. "Ennui," as Alfred de Musset remarked of the nineteenth century, is "the ailment of the age," which neither art nor culture was able to cure. As I suggested earlier, culture cannot be expected to do the work of religion. But this does not mean that a rich cultural life is not an essential element

of life, and may even help sustain—or perhaps help cure—
an individual or a society while it suffers its ailments.

Community is an unequivocal value word in the counter
cultural lexicon, but its reality is very equivocal. The desire
for community is in opposition to the violent noncommunal
ethos of much of American life. Despite the unique vanity
Americans display about being American, communal feeling
is weak. A counter culture proponent, Philip Slater (in *The
Pursuit of Loneliness*), sees the anticommunal individualism
of American society as its besetting vice. The counter culture, as he sees it, insists on the primacy of communal values. He has some difficulty with his young anarchist allies,
for whom "doing your own thing" is a major preoccupation.
But he slips out of the difficulty by insisting that the communal feeling in the counter culture is somehow metaphysi-
cally prior to "doing your own thing," which is no more than
a hangover from the old culture. Slater sees the counter culture as simultaneously emphasizing the "recapturing [of]
direct, immediate, and uncontaminated bodily and sensory
experience" and having a true feeling for the American past:
"The Old West, Amerindian culture, the simple life, the
Utopian community—all venerable American traditions." [13]
The old culture by contrast is rootless, technology minded,
and future oriented. Slater's need to give the counter culture
a feeling for tradition as part of his argument for community leads him to patent falsification and sophistry.*

* This is not to say that the communal idea has no reality in the
counter culture. The commune has tried to extend the family beyond
the kinship bond. People live together from motives of friendship
and love, and they also live together to obviate some of the un-
wholesome consequences of bourgeois life. Cooking, child-raising,
and housecleaning are shared, so that women do not have to shoul-
der the major burden. The difficulties of communal living are understandably not the main preoccupation of the counter culture propo-
nents, who are at the stage where it is necessary to accentuate the
positive. A film like *Easy Rider* with its fundamental sympathy for
the counter culture is honest enough to convey in its rendering of a
hippie commune the genuine threats of boredom, irritation, constraint, and aggression in such a community—difficulties that arise
(apart from the existential condition of man) from a minimal con-

"Doing your own thing" is not a superficial phenomenon in the counter culture: it is one of its premises. And the tradition that Slater evokes for the counter culture is an abstraction, which has little to do with the immediacy of counter cultural experience.

II

If we stand back and compare the current radicalism in America with certain expressions of cultural radicalism in England we might see the extent to which the attack on high culture is a local phenomenon, a symptom of deficiencies in the general society. In the work of the English social critics Raymond Williams and Richard Hoggart (particularly that of Williams) one finds a critique of the cultural tradition that has some power and cogency. Its reference is immediately to the English scene, though it intends broader implications. Neither Williams nor Hoggart shows any profound understanding of the particularities of American life (most references to America are in terms of "Americanization" in England) so that we learn very little from them directly about the cultural tradition in America except as what they say has universal validity. What I find most illuminating in their work, however, are the differences implied between England and America both in their descriptions of the English scene (compared with what I know of American life) and in the tone and character of their critique.

The image of contemporary England that emerges is that of an industrial democracy whose character is still largely shaped by its feudal past. In his conclusion to *The Long*

---

ception of community and culture. The mood of the counter culture has recently passed into encounter groups, women's and men's liberation groups, consciousness raising, and so forth. Members of the adult middle class (whatever the political persuasion) have found themselves susceptible to the vaguely communal ethos of the counter culture. It has come to serve the purpose formerly served by psychoanalysis.

Revolution Williams gives a fresh valuation to the familiar story of the Victorian Compromise.

Somewhere in the nineteenth century (though there are earlier signs) the English middle class lost its nerve, socially, and thoroughly compromised with the class it had virtually defeated. Directed personally towards the old system of family status, it adopted as its social ideal a definite class system, blurred at the top but clear below itself. The distinction of public schools from grammar schools led to a series of compromises: in the curriculum, where just enough new subjects were introduced to serve middle-class training, but just enough old subjects kept to preserve the older cultivation of gentlemen; and in social character, where just enough emphasis on the superiority of the whole class was shrewdly mixed with a rigorous training in concepts of authority and service, so that a formal system could be manned and yet not be disturbed . . . The principal tension, in recent English social life, has been the fixed character of the arrived middle class, with its carefully conditioned ways of speaking and behaving, and the later arrivals or those still struggling to arrive. The worst snobberies still come, with an extraordinary self-revealing brashness, from people who, if family were really the social criterion, would be negligible. The compromise takes care of that, for it had included (what the aristocracy was not unwilling to learn) the accolade of respectability on work and especially the making of money by work. This enabled the pattern to be kept mobile, without altering its character.[14]

Williams does not say that what he calls the long revolution of full democratization has been aborted in England. For him, despite all the obstacles and difficulties and at least as of 1966, the revolution is still in process. The role of America in the process of English democratization is ambiguous at best. At one point Hoggart values the "openness" of American society in its manners and human relationships. But the essential role that America plays in the argument is as a danger that besets the process of true democratization. To the extent that America represents "the massification of society" and money values, she constitutes the degradation of true democratic life, as Hoggart and Williams see it. For them democracy involves a redefinition of human life in which the category of class is eliminated and in which function, that is, the kind of work a man does, is seen as only one element in his full humanity. Democracy is the liberation of the creative possibilities of each man. The operative words are "creative," a word to which Williams devotes a great deal of philological energy, and "each man," underlining Williams' anti-elitism. "We should stop the irrelevant discussion of class, of which most of us are truly sick and tired, and let through the more interesting discussion of human differences, between real people and real communities." [15]

Williams is addressing himself to an English or perhaps European problem. The process of democratization is not inhibited in America by a preoccupation with class difference. There is poverty and racism in America, but they have only complicated the essentially egalitarian (though noncommunal) ethos of American life, an egalitarianism that too often has money as its common denominator. What inhibits the process of democratization in America is precisely this functional definition of human life. The notorious American question is "what is he worth?"—the implication being that the value of a person can be rendered by his income and by his work. Like all industrial countries, England suffers from this functional definition, but on the testimony of Williams and Hoggart the complicated set of inherited attitudes that define class feeling and behavior still creates most of the social tension and unhappiness in English life.

For Williams and Hoggart the problem is to sort out the unnecessary invidiousness of inherited feeling from what Hoggart calls "the lived-in virtues of the past" in order to inform the democratic process with a vital tradition. It is significant that at the same time that Williams and Hoggart argue for an extension of the cultural franchise to people of all classes and insist on extending the definition of culture to include working class attitudes, feeling and lore that have, in their view, been excluded or distorted by the dominant culture, they are passionate exponents of the vital element in the high cultural tradition. Here they differ from cultural radicals in America, who repudiate high culture because of its "privileged" status. American radicals object not simply to the content of high culture, but to its tones, atmospheres, manners, and attitudes, which constitute, in their view, the mental set of the upper classes.

By extending the cultural franchise and by including elements of, say, "working class culture" in the tradition, changes will inevitably occur in the way in which Shakespeare, Milton, and George Eliot will be understood. Yet Hoggart is careful to oppose any leveling conception of culture, "Young scholars have to be trained to take up . . . advanced work and others trained so that they may go out to teach our language and literature." [16] Williams and Hoggart, scions of working class families, betray neither their working class heritage nor their university education. Hoggart devotes an affectionate essay to his teacher Bonamy Dobrée, an anti-type to Hoggart himself ("an upper middle-class professional and military man"), and in *Culture and Society* Williams echoes Mills's tribute to Coleridge in his praising chapter on the conservatism of T. S. Eliot. Complexity, poise, and tone (one of Hoggart's favorite words) are recurrent categories of value. And they both react against vulgarity (a term they try to define against prevailing snobbish standards) with a passion that shows attachment to high cultural values. For them the primary instance of vulgarity is the cultural leveling produced by industrial society.

The fidelity Williams and Hoggart show both to their lower class origins and to their formal education is not fortuitous. On the evidence of Hoggart's *The Uses of Literacy* the ethos of English working class life (before the assault by modern technology) was congenial to high cultural values. Intellectual and imaginative values existed in "working class culture," so that Hoggart's desire to read English at Leeds, for instance, represented a fulfillment rather than a betrayal of his working class origins. (In this connection, one should recall Leavis' insistence on the cultural richness of English provincial life, which nurtured the imaginations of George Eliot, Thomas Hardy, and D. H. Lawrence.)

The American situation is by and large quite different. A serious literary education in America is generally discontinuous with the general purposes of American life—in which men tend to be functionally defined. A liberal education has been largely irrelevant to the technological dynamism of American life. Its original intention was to supply the necessary graces for that odd creature, the American gentleman. More recently, it has been a valuable item in the curricula vitae of applicants for administrative positions with corporations looking for "refined" executives. It is inconceivable that an American radical would write as Hoggart writes of the public value of a liberal education in the following manner. "But before we enjoy a ritual laugh at senior civil servants trained only in the Classics we ought to reflect—as we will if we have worked closely with some of these men— that, whatever its limits, Greats did give the best men the ability to consider issues broadly and disinterestedly. This is not merely a wry comment. That kind of grasp is not automatically acquired with a knowledge of the Two Cultures; it needs to be specifically helped to develop." [17]

Together Williams and Hoggart express the cultural attitudes of anti-Establishment intellectuals, who have their roots in the working class. But they are not describing or representing a counter culture. It is evident from everything they have written that they have a natural sense of community with general English society, which by contrast underlines the sectarianism and wishfulness of the American counter cultural community (wishfulness, because the counter culture tends to confuse the desire for community with the reality of community).

Williams, for instance, devotes many pages in *The Long Revolution* to an analysis of the distribution of the vote between the Labour and the Conservative parties. A comparable interest in the electoral system on the part of a radical in the United States would be considered disgraceful in the movement. It is not enough to say that Williams, after all, has a party that represents the proletarian interest whereas no such major party exists in America. As Williams himself is fully aware, the socialism of the Labour party is bankrupt in idea and in practice. The reason for Williams' interest in the electoral system is twofold: (1) unlike his radical counterpart in America, he is interested in finding out what the actual sentiments of the English working class are, and (2) for all his quarrels with the Establishment he implicitly and deeply believes that he exists in a community, however troubled it might be. Both he and Hoggart argue against class feeling in England; the tone of the argument is marked by the absence of resentment, which indicates that they at least have reached a vantage point of liberated disinterestedness. In the enlightened tradition of Victorian social criticism, Williams and Hoggart are committed to persuasion as well as to other forms of nonviolent militancy. "The most remarkable facts about the British working-class movement, since its origin in the Industrial Revolution, are its conscious and deliberate abstention from general violence, and its firm faith in other methods of advance. These characteristics of the British working class have not always been welcome to its more romantic advocates, but they are a real human strength and a precious inheritance." [18] Nothing of what they write suggests the Armageddon of the American radical imagination.* Perhaps they misrepresent true radical feeling in England. It seems to me rather that the feeling of community is real in England as it is not in America, and the sense of community is temporal as well as spatial. "I agree with Leavis," Williams writes, "as with Coleridge and Arnold and with Burke [note the political character of the writers with whom Williams is in agreement here] . . . that a society is poor indeed if it has nothing to live by but by its

---

* The war in Vietnam has created an exceptional situation in American life. But much of the radical feeling in America cannot be derived simply from the war, and will not go away when the war ends. This should not at all be construed as an argument against the feeling. On the contrary, our grotesque performance in Vietnam has revealed an antecedent condition in American life that alone justifies a radical response. The trauma to the American conscience will not pass—indeed must not pass quickly.

own immediate and contemporary experience." [19] The note of community that Williams strikes is as deep as his radicalism.*

Indeed, this sense of community provides a vantage point from which destructive tendencies in society can be criticized and attacked. As I have already remarked, the distinction of English social and cultural criticism consists partly in its possession of a vital communal consciousness ("the whole way of life"), which it brought to bear in evaluating the signs of the times. Thus, for instance, it could perceive the noxiousness of the commercial element of English society in the nineteenth century in the light of the full spiritual and bodily interests of English culture. In contrast, commercial culture in America, it is felt, is not simply an element in a larger environment as it was in England in the nineteenth century, but is the peculiar genius of American life. Revolutionary sentiment against American society arises in part from the feeling that its very genius is corrupt and "the whole way of life" has to be created anew. Whether the genius of American society is exclusively its commercialism, what the sources of a new communal consciousness are or should be are difficult and as yet unanswered questions. The presumption of the counter culture is the belief that it has the answers, which are simply instinctive in the bodies and desires of those who live the counter culture.

It could be argued that Williams' sense of community is a disability in a radical, that radicalism that respects the rights and even to an extent the vision of the adversary hardly deserves its label. This is doubtless the way American cultural radicals would argue. The truth is that the character of radicalism in a particular society is a function of the character and quality of a given society. In a sense, every society gets the radicalism it deserves. Nobody has stated the problem

* In America, Paul Goodman strikes a comparable note—and he has been significantly misunderstood. His insistence on his conservatism is not capricious. A book that has profoundly influenced him is Coleridge's *On the Constitution of Church and State*—a most unradical book!

better than Joseph Conrad in his introductory note to his novel about Russia before the revolution, *Under Western Eyes.* "The most terrifying reflection (I am speaking now for myself) is that all these people are not the product of the exceptional but of the general—of the normality of their place, and time, and race. The ferocity and imbecility of an autocratic rule rejecting all legality and in fact basing itself upon complete moral anarchism provokes the no less imbecile and atrocious answer of a purely Utopian revolutionism encompassing destruction by the first means to hand, in the strange conviction that a fundamental change of hearts must follow the downfall of any given human institution. These people are unable to see that all they can effect is merely a change of names. The oppressors and the oppressed are all Russians together; and the world is brought once more face to face with the truth of the saying that the tiger cannot change his stripes nor the leopard his spots."

Nevertheless, Conrad is unduly pessimistic. A reaction against a system is in part a free and reflective act, and the possibility of genuine change is real. (The institutions that created British freedom, which Conrad so admired, did not exist immemorially.) If the tiger can change its stripes (not merely the turrets and the citadels, to change the metaphor) it might be essential that those who want change, whether they call themselves radical or not, should resist the temptations of a merely symptomatic role.

The Humanities and Personal Knowledge

If the counter culture has failed to achieve a genuine alternative culture, its "high cultural" adversaries have lost their authority by default. And for a simple reason: much of what has passed for university education has been indefensible. The radical philistinism of recent years has had its adversary counterpart in the academic philistinism of much longer duration. In the humanities and elsewhere this philistinism has presented itself in the guise of scientific detachment and objectivity, which, as I will argue in this chapter, has at once depersonalized and deintellectualized humanistic study. Indeed, I am struck by the frequency with which young radical critics identify the intellectual enterprise with pedantry. The reason, I would conjecture, is that universities rarely offer a lively alternative experience of the intellectual life.

Some time ago, before the radicalization of the university atmosphere, in a class discussion of Matthew Arnold's "The Study of Poetry," a gifted student of mine surprised me with the question: "Is Arnold really a critic?" The student was willing to concede that Arnold might be something else, but the title of critic seemed reserved for another kind of performer. It took very little reflection for me to realize that the student's question came out of the training he had received as a student of literature. He had been well trained in the modern idea of criticism, having been taught the importance of method, its rigorous application, and of course a decent respect for evidence. Arnold's intuitions about the nobility, the sincerity, the high seriousness of the lines he adduced as touchstones of great poetry seemed arbitrary, unsupported by the kind of reasoning and documentation my student had learned to regard as marks of good criticism.

I replied that Arnold's failure to be convincing (to him) might have to do with the inherent elusiveness of judicial criticism: one could possibly prove an interpretation, but an evaluation rooted in taste and the affections is not amenable to proof. It was a reasonable answer, but my response ran counter to the characteristic professional insistence that a student make reasoned assertions and support those assertions by ample reference to the text. Indeed, it was as if the tables had been turned. One of the familiar challenges to a literary education is that of the naive freshman who during the year gains for a brief moment the courage to express his exasperation with the discussion: "All this analysis just spoils the whole enjoyment of the work." If he has some knowledge of the literary tradition he might even cite Wordsworth's phrase, "we murder to dissect." To the instructor caught up in the activity of analysis, there are few things more annoying than the exasperation of the freshman. The student may be simply covering up an inability to follow the discussion. He may prefer without reason or conviction the easy delights of the "experience" of literature. In any event, he is often inarticulate in his own defense, and it is a fairly easy matter—or it used to be a fairly easy matter, until the student demand for relevance gained its present authority—to isolate him from the sympathies of the rest of the class and put him down, as the instructor has to, if he is to get on with his business. What the instructor may say is that our enjoyment is enhanced by analysis, that though it is true that the analysis of a text often becomes autonomous, an exercise without reference to the principal task of criticism (the discovery of the power or the weakness of a work), the good critic makes his analysis relevant to his evaluative purposes.

The gifted student may have been at one time the naive freshman. Had he been served right by being told to forget his enjoyment and learn to analyze texts? The complaint of the freshman, it seems to me, has a serious radical implication for which the instructor's authoritative dismissal fails to account. The implication is that there is a disjunction between analysis and evaluation. The analysis of the structure or pattern of imagery of a work may convince us that the work has unity or ingenuity, but it rarely convinces us that it has the kind of vitality to which we might give the name power or beauty or charm. Indeed, a mediocre or uninteresting poem may be shown to have unity or ingenuity or complexity. We often perceive the power or beauty or charm of a work before the act of analysis, and the analysis may simply assure us that our affections are not misplaced. I am aware that in the act of analysis we sometimes discover the beauty of the thing, but I am not at all convinced that this discovery is caused by the analysis: it may simply be simultaneous with it. T. S. Eliot's analogy is suggestive: "The chief use of the 'meaning' of a poem, in the ordinary sense, may be (for here again I am speaking of some kinds of poetry and not all) to satisfy one habit of the reader, to keep his mind diverted and quiet, while the poem does its work upon him: much as the imaginary burglar is always provided with a bit of nice meat for the house-dog." [1]

In any event, I think it indisputable that there are matters central to our experience of literature (like the beauty of an image or the eloquence of a statement or the magnificence of a character) that cannot be inferred from any analysis, no matter how ingenious the method. By what method can we establish the greatness of Tolstoy's sentence: "Ivan Ilych's life had been the most simple and most ordinary and therefore most terrible"? It is a great sentence; it has truth, simplicity, and a resonance that makes it classic. But in saying this I am not analyzing the sentence or proving my claim for it. I am doing what any critic has to do: I am pointing to a great moment in a work and isolating it, so that it can be contemplated and enjoyed. (The sentence of course has a paradoxical quality: one does not expect "most terrible" after "most ordinary" and "most simple." But to point out the paradox is not to indicate the greatness of the statement.)

I do not mean to encourage a facile impressionism or a self-indulgent expression of likes and dislikes as the substance of serious literary discussion. In the uncultivated mind impressionistic criticism becomes visceral response. The insistence on the experience of literature often excludes the role of mind in that experience. The stress on personal engagement has other dangers. The student becomes interested only in what he considers to be relevant to fashionable concerns and the result can be an impoverishment of sensibility and knowledge. Moreover, the assumption that the student knows what is relevant to him is often unfounded. One of the main purposes of an education is the opportunity it gives the student to cast about in the past, so that he can both find and form his intellectual and moral identity. The capacity to suspend belief and disbelief, an element in the scientific attitude, is essential to a literary education.

The fact remains, however, that the commitment to analysis over against evaluation has been a permanent professorial posture, indifferent to the sophistications and needs of the students.

The commitment to analysis derives from the generally covert, sometimes overt, sympathy that exists between criticism and its nineteenth century enemy, technology (misnamed science by nineteenth century critics). The "progress" of criticism in this century has been roughly analogous to the development of technology. The practicing modern critic (like the technologist) is proud of his methods and techniques. He might even claim (with the technological scientist) that more progress has been made in the technology of his discipline during the past fifty years than in its entire previous history. The cult of the method is so strong that even critics whose mode is primarily intuitive and impressionist cannot resist using the word method to characterize their activity. The view is connected with a thoroughly professional outlook. Without a method to motivate the critical act, criticism is doomed to a hopeless impressionism, to

54

statements of likes and dislikes that can hardly pass into genuine intellectual discourse. The twentieth century critic has
implicitly or explicitly accepted the authority of technology in
our culture.

Indeed, the extraordinary prestige of Northrop Frye results from his bold and erudite attempt to liberate criticism
from its "prehistoric" attitude. The following are statements
from his *Anatomy of Criticism.* "Criticism seems to be
badly in need of a coordinating principle, a central hypothe-
sis which, like the theory of evolution in biology, will see the
phenomena it deals with as parts of a whole. The first postu-
late of this inductive leap is the same as that of any science:
the assumption of total coherence. Simple as this assumption
appears, it takes a long time for a science to discover that it
is in fact a totally intelligible body of knowledge." "The first
step in developing a genuine poetics is to recognize and get
rid of meaningless criticism, or talking about literature in a
way that cannot help to build up a systematic structure of
knowledge. This includes all the sonorous nonsense that we
often find in critical generalities, reflective comments, ideological perorations, and other consequences of taking a large
view of an unorganized subject." "The accuracy of any critic's
good taste is no guarantee that its inductive basis in literary experience is adequate. This may still be true even
after the critic has learned to base his judgements on his experience of literature and not on his social, moral, religious,
or personal anxieties." [2] Frye has brought to the surface
what has always been the half-concealed fantasy of modern
criticism.

The methodological or "scientific" view is pervasive both
in the teaching of literature and the writing of criticism. It
has its enemies, some of whom are our best critics, but it is
in the very nature of the opposition that no systematic or co-
herent case is made against the methodologists. Yet the case
should be made, for the deficiencies in contemporary literary
education cannot be remedied by an increased dosage of
what students already receive in large quantity: method,

technique. Lionel Trilling, a cultural critic who has resisted the claims of the methodologists, is very sensitive to the loss of engagement incurred by modern "methods." Modern criticism "has taught us how to read certain books; it has not taught us how to engage them. Modern literature (it need scarcely be said again) is directed toward moral and spiritual renovation; its doctrine is damnation and salvation. It is a literature of doctrine, which, although often concealed, is very aggressive. The occasions are few when criticism has met this doctrine on its own fierce terms. Of modern criticism it can be said that it has instructed us in an intelligent passivity before the beneficent aggression of literature. Attributing to literature virtually angelic powers, it has passed the word to readers of literature that the one thing you do not do when you meet an angel is wrestle with him." [3] Trilling advocates the engagement with literature that inevitably leads to "critical generalities, reflective comments, ideological perorations," to use Frye's scornful rhetoric.

The case for a nonmethodological criticism, especially where judgment is concerned, is implicit in the nineteenth century critics who waged war on all forms of mechanistic thinking, indeed, who saw the very life of literature (which included criticism) in the preservation of vital, organic modes of thought against the usurping tendencies of the machine. It is implicit in Arnold's concept of "the real estimate," which he distinguishes from other forms of criticism: the personal and the historical.

The task of the judicial critic (the highest type of critic, in Arnold's view) is to possess "the best that has been known and thought" and derive from them standards of perfection against which the rest of literature can be judged. The touchstones are great lines or moments in these works, symbols of their power. To make these touchstones truly inward is to have come into full possession of literary culture in its highest expressions. The work of a real estimate is the finding of touchstones and the use of them to judge other works of literature.

There are undeniable difficulties in Arnold's doctrine. The New Criticism has been specially sensitive to Arnold's willingness to disintegrate the whole work ("the organic whole") into individual lines. It is of course true that individual lines get their power and resonance from the context, though I think it a New Critical excess to disallow poetic power to individual lines. (The resonance of Tolstoy's sentence is independent of its context, its being the opening sentence of the second chapter of *The Death of Ivan Ilych*.) Moreover, Arnold's sharp separation of the three kinds of critical estimate (the personal, the historical, and the real) gives a misleading picture of the actual operation of the critical faculty. Arnold's own performance in "The Study of Poetry" shows how even the most discriminating of critics is inevitably swayed by his personal likes and dislikes and is determined often without his knowing it by his own historical situation. Arnold's notorious exclusion of Chaucer from the ranks of the supremely great (because he lacks "high seriousness") reveals Arnold's rather than Chaucer's limitations: a high Victorian solemnity which made him insensitive to comedy and gaiety in literature. And nothing in Arnold's doctrine can correct this "mistaken" judgment, because the touchstones ineluctably represent the combined effort of the personal response, the historical consciousness of the critic, and the attempt to find universal qualities.

What this means is that the act of establishing touchstones involves a critical act the very opposite of what Arnold himself advocated. Literature is not simply a criticism of life, but is itself to be criticized by life. The books one chooses to live by are not dictated merely by other books, but by one's experience, one's sense of life as well. Literature as a criticism of life is complemented, not superseded, by the criticism one makes of literature on the basis of one's experience of life. In that sense the richer and the more intelligent one's experience of life (moral, political, aesthetic, spiritual) the richer one's experience of literature.

Nevertheless, the concept of a *real* estimate has value. Arnold makes two characteristic statements in "The Study of Poetry": "If we are thoroughly penetrated by their [the touchstones'] power, we shall find that we have acquired a sense enabling us, whatever poetry may be laid before us, to feel the degree in which a high poetical quality is present or wanting there. Critics give themselves great labour to draw out what in the abstract constitutes the characters of high quality in poetry. It is much better to have recourse to concrete examples;—to take specimens of poetry of the high, the very highest quality, and to say: 'The characters of a high quality of poetry are what is expressed *there*.'" "At any rate the end to which the method and the estimate are designed to lead, and from leading to which, if they do lead to it, they get their whole value,—the benefit of being able clearly to feel and deeply to enjoy, the best, the truly classic in poetry,—is an end, let me say it once more at parting, of supreme importance." 4 The real estimate, in Arnold's view, is no mere description of the object as in itself it really is, but a *possession* of that object of which the great line must be construed as a symbol of the whole work. To possess is to make inward the qualities of nobility, sincerity, variety, suppleness: the qualities that inform great literature. It is not particular qualities that Arnold assigns to literature that I want to stress, but rather the act of possessing the work. Arnold's formula covers a revolutionary conception of literature, which Arnold personally would not have endorsed.

For his conception of culture as an inward state, Arnold is much indebted to John Henry Newman. The affinities between them are particular and numerous; they have their source in the shared sense that contemporary liberalism and culture were in an inimical relation to each other and that the values of culture needed to be fortified. Newman's *Discourses on the Idea of a University* can be regarded not only as an anticipation of Arnold's *Culture and Anarchy,* but as the educational program for the Arnoldian regime of culture. Raymond Williams, in *Culture and Society,* puts the connection very well.5 He quotes from Newman's discourse VII, *On the Scope and Nature of University Education* (1852): "It were well if the English, like the Greek language, possessed some definite word to express, simply and generally, intellectual proficiency or perfection, such as 'health,' as used with reference to the animal frame, and 'virtue' with reference to our moral nature."

After expressing surprise that Newman "does not meet the want of 'some definite word' with the word 'culture,' " Williams notes that Newman in effect announces Arnold's task in *Culture and Anarchy* when he speaks of the consequence of this lack, which makes (in Newman's words) "many words . . . necessary, in order, first, to bring out and convey what is surely no difficult idea in itself—that of the cultivation of the intellect as an end; next, in order to recommend what surely is no unreasonable object; and lastly, to describe and realize to the mind the particular perfection in which that object consists." It is of course true that Newman and Arnold served different gods. For Arnold, culture is an ultimate value, assimilating to itself the spiritual values that have loosened from religious dogma; for Newman, culture is at best the penultimate rung in the hierarchy of values. But this disaffinity in ultimate matters should not divert us from the spiritual-aesthetic sympathies between the two ideas of culture, ideas that seem often translatable into one another. Arnold crystallized in the word culture the values that Newman formulated in the *Idea of a University*. In some respects, Newman's speculations about inward culture go far beyond those of Arnold. More philosophical than Arnold, Newman was aware of the need for an epistemological basis for his theory of culture and education. In the *Grammar of Assent* (1870) he tried to account for the mental conditions of thinking from the earliest assumptions to the assent the mind gives to a proposition. Newman's interest in the problem is in direct contrast to the failure of the utilitarians to recognize that a problem existed. Thus for the utilitarians the assent to truth was an automatic reflex.

A key concept in *The Grammar of Assent* is the concept

of the Illative Sense. The Illative Sense is concrete reasoning, which Newman distinguishes from "mere skill in argumentative science." Because of the subtle and elastic nature of its action, it cannot be incarnated into a method. "In reasoning on any subject, whatever, which is concrete, we proceed, as far indeed as we can, by the logic of language, but we are obliged to supplement it by the more subtle and elastic logic of thought; for forms by themselves prove nothing." The main analogue for the Illative Sense is the living organism to which Newman characteristically opposes the machine. Man's "progress is a living growth, not a mechanism; and its instruments are mental acts [of the Illative Sense], not the formulas and contrivances of language." And again: "It is the mind that reasons, and controls its reasonings, not any technical apparatus of words and propositions. This power of judging and concluding, when in its perfection, I call the Illative Sense." [6] The image of the mind at work is of a human ensemble of faculties willed into motion, not of a machine: "a technical apparatus of words and propositions."

It follows from its human, living quality that the Illative Sense is a personal sense. This has radical implications for intellectual discourse. "One function indeed there is of Logic, to which I have referred in the preceding sentence, which the Illative Sense does not and cannot perform. It supplies no common measure between mind and mind, as being nothing else than a personal gift or acquisition. Few there are, as I said above, who are good reasoners on all subject-matters. Two men, who reason well each in his own province of thought, may, one or both of them, fail and pronounce opposite judgements on a question belonging to some third province. Moreover, all reasoning being from premises, and those premises arising (if it so happen) in their first elements from personal characteristics, in which men are in fact in essential and irremediable variance one with the other, the ratiocinative talent can do no more than point out where the difference between them lies, how far it is immaterial, when it is worth while continuing an argument between them, and when not." [7] Newman protects the Illative Sense from the charge of vulgar subjectivism by insisting on the mental and ratiocinative aspect of the Illative Sense and by defining it normatively as the mind in its perfection. It is neither mystical nor irrational, it comes to life only at the moment that it begins to embody itself in rational discourse. But its reality is not exhausted by the method and logical forms of rational discourse. The Illative Sense should not be confused with the modern idea of "the creative" which is often counterposed to the rational. Newman's insight is that the act of reasoning itself is not to be reduced to mechanistic formulas. This is not to say that logic and method are banished from intellectual discourse. What Newman rejects is the notion that method or methodology can be a significant *motive* for intellectual activity. In Newman's view, the motive for intellectual activity is irreducibly "personal" and "vital." *

For Newman, the Illative Sense is a manifestation of grace. He argues in the traditional Christian manner that the exercise of reason receives its ultimate sanction from God —that reason without grace is bound to go astray. But it is possible to regard the religious implication of the concept as an analogue rather than as strictly necessary. Indeed, Newman's commentators have done him a disservice in insisting on the religious context of *The Grammar of Assent*. Charles Harrold, for instance, says in his introduction to *The Grammar of Assent* that Newman appeals to "those who accept his postulates—the existence of a God, the immortality of the

---

* Newman is in the tradition of English social criticism of the nineteenth century even in such a matter as the Illative Sense— though his ultimate commitments, his inspirations are so different from those of the other great English social critics. Like Carlyle, Ruskin, and Arnold, Newman attacks what Carlyle first described as the usurpation of the spiritual provinces by the machine. His distinction is that he does not succumb to the temptations of an obscurantist mysticism, which one finds in Carlyle and others influenced by German romanticism. Good Catholic that he is, Newman remains squarely in the rationalist tradition. Thus he avoids Carlyle's vulgar identification of the rational with the mechanical and the dynamic with the creative.

soul, the freedom of the will, the existence of sin and virtue, the possibility of a revelation and of a mediator between man and god." [8] Harrold states this immediately after he has paid tribute to Newman's unique and extraordinary capacity to deal with the objections of atheists and agnostics. It is difficult to see how Newman exercises this capacity if he begins with assumptions absolutely unacceptable to atheists and agnostics. On the contrary, Newman (like Pascal) moves very carefully on the empirical plane, deliberately choosing the ground of his antagonist in order to convert him. "We are in a world of facts, and we use them; for there is nothing else to use." [9]

Thus his account of disagreement among historical scholars appeals to one's empirical knowledge of the frequent difficulty, if not impossibility, of arriving at agreement in interpretation and judgment. "Here, I say again, it does not prove that there is no objective truth, because not all men are in possession of it; or that we are not responsible for the associations which we attach, and the relations which we assign, to the objects of the intellect. But this it does suggest to us, that there is something deeper in our differences than the accident of external circumstances; and that we need the interposition of a Power, greater than human teaching and human argument, to make our beliefs true and our minds one." "To make our beliefs true and our minds one": Newman's ultimate interest, it is clear, is to fortify the intellectual respectability of Catholicism, with its dependence on revelation and intuition, against the presumption of an Absolutist reason. But this argument has an important by-product. In the course of showing the necessity of a higher power (which, incidentally, is not the same as proving its existence), Newman gives an accurate description of the relativism of intellectual life: the diversity of cogent, yet often contradictory, viewpoints that exist. We do not have to believe in Newman's God to agree with the following conclusion about the differences among historians of the Roman Empire: "I am not contrasting these various opinions of able men, who have given themselves to historical research, as if it were any reflection on them that they differ from each other. It is the cause of their differing on which I wish to insist. Taking the facts by themselves, probably these authors would come to no conclusion at all; it is the 'tacit understandings' which Mr. Grote speaks of, the vague and impalpable notions of 'reasonableness' on his own side as well as that of others, which both make conclusions possible, and are the pledge of their being contradictory. The conclusions vary with the particular writer, for each writes from his own point of view and with his own principles, and these admit of no common measure." [10]

I have called attention to Newman's concept of the Illative Sense because it is an illuminating metaphor for those elusive and spontaneous movements of the mind that cannot be reduced to methods or logical procedures and are yet themselves the inspiration for methods and logical procedures. The Illative Sense is the first mover, the sustainer of the argumentative process, and the generator of assent. It "has its function in the beginning, middle and end of all verbal discussion and Inquiry, and in every step of the process." [11] The Illative Sense operates in all intellectual endeavors. Newman's major instances are from history, but he argues for the position in the sciences as well. Its largest role, however, would seem to be reserved for the humanities and, one would suppose, for literary study in particular. Even if it is true that the advances of logic and psychology constantly make inroads into the territory of the Illative Sense, the concept is useful as a symbol of an alternative to a mechanistic conception of thinking. It implies that the basis of civilized intelligence is something more profound and inclusive than the mental machine modern rationalism has constructed. The Illative Sense is too subtle and multiform to be measured by rule, because it is nothing less than the product of the whole man, the ensemble of faculties and circumstances that go into the making of his total being.

For Newman the Illative Sense in its perfection leads to

Truth, to a community if not an identity of mind with others who have achieved a similar perfection. For the relativist (which comprises most of us) the Illative Sense in its perfection (if we could employ the concept) would be the enrichment and clarification of each one's sense of truth—though it might be difficult, if not in certain cases impossible, to achieve that common measure with the senses of truth that others have. There exists the possibility for each one to perfect his own sense of truth.

The argument for the personal character of knowledge has been made recently and most impressively by Michael Polanyi. Though Polanyi is strictly outside the religious tradition and vocabulary—indeed, he is postreligious as well as postcritical—his argument is reminiscent of Newman's *The Grammar of Assent,* despite the fact that he makes no reference to it. Thus he attacks the objectivist presumption of the digital computer in its "sustained effort to eliminate what are called 'psychological' elements—the factors which I call 'tacit.' " [12] Polanyi believes this to be impossible because there remains "an irreducible residue of mental operations, on which the operation of the formalized system itself will continue to rely." For instance, "the acceptance of a mark on paper as a symbol implies that (a) we believe that we can identify the mark in various instances of it and (b) that we know its proper symbolic use. In both these beliefs we may be mistaken, and they constitute therefore commitments of our own." What Polanyi calls "the tacit dimension" is roughly equivalent to Newman's Illative Sense—which is prior to logic and articulateness but by no means incompatible with them. The difference between Newman and Polanyi (a notable one for the modern sensibility) is that Polanyi's concept of personal knowledge is utterly without absolutist implications. The person, for Polanyi, under no circumstances speaks with the authority of God. For Polanyi, knowledge is at once rational and subjective, real (possessing an intrinsic or existential meaning) and yet personal and relative. The "logic of affirmation" is in the liberation from objectivism:

"To realize that we can voice our ultimate convictions only from within our convictions—from within the whole system of acceptances that are logically prior to any particular assertion of our own, prior to the holding of any particular piece of knowledge. If an ultimate logical level is to be attained and made explicit, this must be a declaration of my personal beliefs. I believe that the function of philosophic reflection consists in bringing to light, and affirming as my own, the beliefs implied in such of my thoughts and practice as I believe to be valid." [13]

Recent attacks on the objectivist illusion of scientists by critics who are themselves committed to the value of the scientific enterprise add force to an argument such as the one that Polanyi makes in *Personal Knowledge*. In *The Structure of Scientific Revolutions* Thomas Kuhn is at pains to show the personal, historical, and sociological factors that establish and give authority to a particular paradigm—in short, factors that are contingent and accidental from an objectivist point of view. He also shows how the paradigm in a sense creates the facts that validate it and how it excludes facts that might undermine its validity. It is important to emphasize (against distorting uses of Kuhn's work) that Kuhn does not make his argument for the partial or relative character of any given scientific paradigm in a contentious and nihilistic spirit. He does not mean to foster a corrosive skepticism with regard to claims made by scientists for the validity of the paradigm to which they subscribe. On the contrary, he sees in the scrupulous relativism of scientists the progressive vitality of science.

If the personal element is important in the natural and social sciences, how much more important it must be in the humanities. One explanation for the passion for objectivity that one sometimes finds among humanists is that the prominence of the personal element embarrasses the humanist when he thinks of himself as engaged in a discipline. By suppressing the personal element he believes that he has increased the "scientific" value of his work. But if the personal element exists in the sciences as an inevitable and in some ways fortunate condition then the effort to suppress the personal element may turn out to be, paradoxically, unscientific.

I myself am not so attached to the term science in humanistic study that I would want to argue for the personal element in the humanities in the name of science. I do believe strongly in the value of rational discourse and empirical evidence and would quarrel with any conception of humanistic study that would exploit the personal element to justify mindless impressionism. But it seems to me that the central failure of humanistic study in America and elsewhere is the failure to perceive the necessary relation between personal response and appropriation and the rational structure that articulates and justifies it. When a teacher imposes an impersonal method of study on a class he is not fostering the only knowledge that matters, that is, the knowledge that becomes personal. If he does by chance foster such knowledge, it is because the method has accidentally attached itself to the curiosities of the students.

Better by far is the effort of the teacher to assert his view of a subject as coherently and as lucidly as possible, making clear at the same time, so far as he is able, the limitations and vulnerabilities of his position—in other words, making clear that his view is personal, thereby creating openings for students to assert their own views. The only demand imposed upon all personal views is that they be articulated as fully and as logically as possible. The "progressive" or "radical" idea that the teacher surrender or suspend his personality so that the personal views of the students can come forth leads too often to the prizing of expression for the sake of expression—however banal, incoherent, or uninteresting it may be. The progressive idea often takes the form of a direct relationship between teacher and student, unmediated by method, text, or even intellect. The classroom becomes an occasion for an encounter group or a "bull session." The vice of unmediated person to person "relating" (one can scarcely call it teaching) is the opposite vice to that of a methodologically motivated pedagogy. What I am arguing for is not a compromise, but an understanding of the true relationship between the personal and the methodological.

It should be clear that the value of the personal element is not simply heuristic—that is, to entertain or interest the student. It goes to the very heart of the humanist enterprise—which is to satisfy, in Arnold's words, the instinct for moral conduct and the desire for beauty and, one might add, the formation of intellect. The humanities are, after all, about the person.

To be sure, an education that seriously tries to engage the personal element is, practically speaking, on very difficult ground. The methodologists may well ask: if the mind is as subtle, multiform, and elastic in its movements as Newman claims, how can the many different minds that must be educated be controlled for the purposes of education? Modern methodologists can plausibly argue that education be concerned with what is public and manageable: logic, method, procedure. It is no accident I think that the widespread demand for methods among educators comes at a time when higher education is becoming democratic—a possibility for everyone. The strength of the methodologists is that their program serves the democratic interest in providing a basis for education for everybody willing to learn: it also has the corollary (though less attractive) "virtues" of creating a vessel, so to speak, for the transmission of established ideas and notions and of providing intellectual security for the teacher.

I have no adequate answer to the argument for method in the practical situation. The danger of mindless impressionism in humanistic study is sufficiently clear. Indeed, if one stresses the importance of the personal element, one must at the same time insist on the personal assertion that can achieve the authority of articulateness, coherence, and insight: in Newman's language, the Illative Sense in its perfection. The very danger of mindless impressionism in intellectual life—that every opinion has equal value—inevitably makes elitism a necessary condition of valuing the personal response.* Of course, the aristocratic or elitist implication that only the graced are truly educable is a further irritant to the methodologists. By suppressing the theme of personality in intellectual life one creates an equality of opportunity before the Method. And yet one must ask the methodologists if their achievement or hopes for achievement amount to an education.

Certainly if one regards the evaluative function of criticism as an important if not the most important function of criticism, the challenge to the methodologists is a formidable one. For no method can create the necessary relation between incisively articulate personality and the work, a relation that makes for interesting evaluations.

Most practical criticism takes for granted the heritage of judgments and tries to understand and interpret what has already been evaluated as worthy. Few critics are called to the judicial function, and those who exercise it without genuine authority seem pretentious, arbitrary, or absurd. The division of labor is perhaps the inevitable result of the extraordinary talent and character necessary for judicial criticism. In the history of literature, judicial criticism has usually been exercised by creative writers who have responded to works past and present out of their authority as artists. When T. S. Eliot argues in "Tradition and the Individual Talent" that each genuinely new work involved a remaking of the literary tradition, he was characterizing the judicial aspect of creative work. Thus at one point in the history of modern literature, Eliot was compelled to elevate the metaphysical poets above Milton, because an interest in Donne was more nourishing to the vitality of modern poetry than an interest in Milton. A judicial critic like F. R. Leavis, whose base is academic, is something of an anomaly, but even he can be

* An open university, devoted to a higher education for everyone, will necessarily have to compromise on the matter of height. But it does not follow that the necessary compromises jeopardize the education of those capable of and willing to achieve an "elitest" education, to use a disreputable though not discredited word.

accounted for by the large part of his character that is rooted outside a strictly academic environment and forms the moral interest of his work.

Though there are legitimate reasons for this division of labor, we are not required to accept it as the ultimate condition of literary study nor are we required to accept it in its present extreme form. The gap between evaluation and analysis or interpretation is to a large extent the product of a dissociation of our literary responses, sanctioned by modern critical theory and ritualized by the educational system. The acquiring of a critical method to mediate one's response to literature is in a sense a refuge from the difficult task of discovering one's own cultivated personal response to a work as the basis of significant literary discourse. The habit of living, intelligent introspection about one's reading and experiences is precisely what Arnold means by culture as the pursuit of perfection and what Newman means by the exercise of the Illative Sense.

The assumption of the impersonality of true knowledge carries into the professional view of what a work of art is. Since Eliot critics have never tired of insisting on the impersonality of works of art. What Eliot meant is a complicated matter—and I do not intend here to reconstruct the logic of his position. It is enough to say that he did not mean to assert that art had no relation to the personality of the creator. He saw the work of art as a kind of self-overcoming, as representing a self not necessarily continuous with the daily biographical self. What contemporary criticism does is simply ignore the personality of the work. The work is not seen as an act of personal will, an expression of self—so that the critic cannot put himself in relation of a person to another person. He encounters the work as an object, which he interprets without judgments, anger, indignation, or passion. As a reader, of course, he cannot avoid these feelings (and they may even be stated), but strictly speaking they do not belong to the economy of the critical act. The object, to be sure, often resonates with transcendental significance because it is

Art, but like a transcendental object in the religious sphere it is regarded as blasphemy to assume a personal attitude toward it. If there is a personal element in the response, it concerns the feeling of humility or inadequacy of the reader in the presence of the transcendental object.

The *lecteur idéal* of the inherited system of education is the Joycean parody of the ideal reader, whose first experience of a work is the feeling of intimidation and who learns to serve it in every conceivable way. He is the reader whom Joyce half-jokingly dreamed of, who devotes a lifetime to the understanding of the intention of say *Ulysses* or *Finnegans Wake* with the single-minded devotion of a communicant and who never conceives the idea or desire to resist anything he studies. He develops a gift for "close reading," a rather obscure phrase, which in effect often means the fitting of what is read into a preformed system or method. He acquires the habit of thinking exclusively within the decorum or idiom of another mind and this habit enervates his capacity to make evaluations. Anyone who has done a survey of Joycean criticism and scholarship knows exactly what I mean. Essays and books are given over to the puzzling out of intricacies in the work (or in the mind of the scholar) without any attempt to evaluate the significance or interest of these intricacies. They may, for instance, be simply boring. The task of the scholar or critic, in such a view, is purely exegetical. His text is his bible and while he is working on the text, the text has no boundaries, no limitations. To resist it wholly or in any part would be an act of irreverence.

The situation has changed somewhat during the past half-decade or so—but only superficially. It has been the habit of the university until recently to resist changes in literary attitude and fashion and to accept them reluctantly only when they become irresistible. This has been the conservative function of the academy, and it has suited the temperamental timidity and insecurity of academicians. The academy, now in breathless pursuit of the contemporary, tries to anticipate the future. Academic journals devoted to the contemporary apply "the method" that had been previously reserved for canonized work. But this does not mean that the academic habit has essentially changed. What we have now is a kind of intimidation in which very little is resisted out of fear that the academy will be found unresponsive. To resist the new now requires the kind of courage that was formerly demanded by an appreciation of the new.

If literature, as nineteenth century critics believed, is still concerned with the human element (ideally with the whole man) in a technological age, then it would seem that criticism itself would betray literature by adopting technological modes of operation. How, for instance, does the methodological critic deal with a literature that attacks his fundamental convictions? How does he respond to the perversities of Dostoevsky's underground man, the narcissism of Genet, the cult of sterility in Beckett? The critic with the capacity to absorb all experiences is simply suspending his disbelief and engaging in an objective analysis of texts. He may fault the writer for technical failures, but he accepts the work as part of his literary experience indiscriminately.

The view that thought and expression in a work of art are inseparable might suggest that an offensive or untrue thought would diminish the work. But the consequences modern critics draw is that the art (the form or style or any other aesthetic category) mitigates, conceals, or neutralizes the offensiveness or falsity of the thought by making irrelevant the question of its morality or truth. This is why the reader is supposed to suspend willingly his disbelief. From an indifference to the question of truth, it is a small step to an implicit assent to the "truth" of the artistic statement. A good analogue is the characteristic response to television commercials: the medium is the message.

What is too often missing in the modern critical response is what the work itself demands: an intelligent assertion of the self (the humanistic critical self) vis-à-vis the work. This dialectical encounter between critic and the work of literature may result in a rejection of the work or a conviction born of personal experience and reflection that the vision of life contained in the book is false or menacing, or it may result in an inner struggle in which the power of the work cannot be entirely resisted and the reader surrenders to it, partially or fully.

It is not enough for the critic to be informed, intelligent, and critically trained. He must turn to account his personal history—his moral, political, and spiritual interests, his experience of people, his characteristic relationship to people, his historical identity. He encounters literature not simply as a specialist, but as one in possession of his humanity, fragmentary and distorted as it may be: accepting, resistant, indifferent by turns. "All criticism," Roland Barthès * has justly remarked, "must include in its discourse . . . an implicit discussion of itself; for to rephrase a play of words by Claudel, criticism is knowledge of the other and co-naissance [a pun on knowledge and birth] of oneself in the world." [14]

* I am here making somewhat illicit use of Barthès—whose criticism is methodological in the pejorative sense in which I understand the term. But if Barthès' own work does not satisfy the demand of his valuable statement, it does not render the statement any the less valuable.

Literary Study and Radicalism

The cult of objectivity with its false assumption that one can approach a literary text without personal motives or that one can fruitfully neutralize these motives has had a negative effect on criticism and scholarship. Radicals who have not taken the anti-intellectualist way of opting for a counter culture have found in some version of Marxism the basis for an attack on the established methods. Presumably Marxism will supply them with a new ideological basis for criticism and scholarship. But so far the work of the "radical conscience" in literary studies has been largely destructive.

In an essay on "The Teaching of Literature in the Highest Academies of the Empire," Bruce Franklin, a professor at Stanford, attacks both the profession and professor for showing an aesthetic and scholarly indifference to the sufferings of the masses and the political issues of the day. He sees the condition of the profession as expressing the stage of capitalism in which we are presently living, as performing its "historic mission" of shaping counterrevolutionary values.

He is white and he is male. When he works, he wears a tie and a jacket. He makes $14,000 a year for nine months work. He teaches one and a half hours a day . . . He believes that he is one of the most intelligent people in the world . . . He believes that he belongs to no particular social class, or at least that he has no particular class interest. He believes that great literature, like himself, stands outside social classes and their sordid struggles, commenting upon them with an Olympian overview. That is why he is worth even more money than he gets. He is the scholar-critic-professor of literature.

This ignorant, self-deceived parasite, perfect butt of the satire he so admires, does indeed have an important role in the twilight hour of the dictatorship of the bourgeoisie . . . Only a totalitarian state would expect people to read Mao, who tells them they are the real heroes of history and that "it is right to rebel" because the earth belongs to the people. Only a highly civilized professor would compel people to read T. S. Eliot who tells them that they are trash stuffed with straw, or Jonathan Swift, who tells them they are shit-smeared monkeys.

How should great literary art be studied? Why, it should be studied in what is called "its own terms." It should be studied as a privately created world essentially independent of the social and political context within which it developed.

Then there is the relation between human "nature" and art. The primary assumption is that human "nature" has always been, and will always remain, essentially the same. It follows from this that literature is timeless. The most essential quality of this human "nature" is that it's incorrigibly corrupt. The greatest works of literature are therefore hopeless, grotesque, tragic or absurd. Hopeful works are silly, naive, or, to use the most revealing term, sentimental. Good characters are often unbelievable, but no character is too evil to believe. Desdemona is something of an embarrassment. Iago is not only credible but fascinating. Only Dr. Pangloss or one of Pope's dunces could agree with Mao that "the masses are the real heroes." [1]

These quotations hardly do justice to the article. The rest of the article is more of the same, but its power is in its cumulative effect, which mere quotation cannot possibly render. I should say at once that the article did not appear in a radical journal, but in one of the most established of establishment journals, *College English.*

Is there any truth in this diatribe? It is true that the dominant tradition of literary study has been the New Criticism, which in its purest expression isolates the work from its time and place, and that one effect of this isolation was to depoliticize the work. My own sense of the critical enterprise has always been at odds with the New Criticism, so that I am not defending it when I say that there is more to the New Critical position than Franklin's vulgar reduction of it would seem to indicate and that Franklin patently falsifies aspects of New Criticism. The New Criticism was fostered by political conservatives (who were concerned with the political dimension of their literary criticism—see Eliot's essays, see Tate's *Reactionary Essays*), but it was not exclusively developed by conservatives (see Richards, Leavis, Empson, whom Franklin admires, possibly because of Empson's sympathies with Mao). Anyone reading Empson, for instance, on ambiguity or on the pastoral can see how an imaginative attention to the text can move out to considerations beyond the text itself. Whatever the shortcomings of New Critical theory and practice (which were often drastic), the habit of looking carefully and imaginatively at what was actually happening in a work of art was a valuable habit, which the New Criticism fostered and developed.

Franklin's view of the professional literary assumption of the relation between human nature and art, to the extent that it makes sense, is blatant distortion. How could modern critics who read and admire Blake or Wordsworth deduce the proposition from literature that human nature is incorrigibly corrupt? Most eighteenth century writers (including Alexander Pope, for whom Franklin has no use) do not subscribe to the doctrine of man's sinful nature. Even Christian doctrine does not hold to the incorrigible corruption of human nature, as anyone who has taken the trouble to read with intelligence Augustine's *Confessions*, the poems of George Herbert, or *Paradise Lost* (the work of a revolutionary writer) would be quick to see. What is the meaning of grace and salvation, if man's nature is incorrigibly corrupt? If the tragic and the hopeless are identical, then Shakespeare's imaginative career is an absurdity. It would require too much space to argue for the affirmative element in tragedy, as Aristotle and Nietzsche argued in different ways, in which Yeats believed when he spoke of the gaiety of Hamlet and Lear, for which Shakespeare testified when he developed the comic romance in the last period of his life out of the perception of the positive energies in the tragic worlds of *Hamlet, Lear,*

75

Macbeth, Othello and *Antony and Cleopatra*. Franklin does not have to believe all this, but at the very least he must show an inkling of awareness that these are views held within the profession, and argue with them.

Because he is committed to an a priori view that modern criticism (despite its considerable variety) represents in a fairly monolithic way "the twilight hour of the dictatorship of the bourgeoisie," Franklin is simply not concerned or equipped to study the actual achievements and failures of New Criticism. (That there is a vast amount of pedantic and worthless stuff turned out in the name of New Criticism is beyond question, but then I would consider it unfair to the idea of Marxist literary criticism to judge it by the vulgar and primitive criticism that is often written in the name of Marx.) * Whether the great leader is Mao or Stalin, it is not hard to imagine what new scholarship will come out of a repudiation of contemporary literary study in these terms: "New Criticism, which emerged in the 1930s to halt the advance of proletarian culture, gained complete ascendancy in the early 1950s as part of the triumph of anti-communist ideology." [2]

The manifest incoherence or bad faith of his argument—it is difficult to say which—shows itself in what Franklin chooses to leave out in his account of the practice of literary criticism during the past several decades. During the period when New Criticism gained ascendancy a body of political literary criticism developed, versed in Marx, Engels, Lenin,

---

* Franklin is an instance of vulgarity, but the vulgarity is a characteristic phenomenon of current American radicalism and therefore requires attention. It may be objected that the distance between Franklin and Lukacs for instance is so great that to characterize Franklin's performance as Marxist or radical is a travesty of both terms. Perhaps. In which case the appropriate terms would be pseudo-radical or pseudo-Marxist. In any event, the "pseudo-radicals" and "pseudo-Marxists" have preempted much of the radical territory and there doesn't seem much corrective response from the "genuine" radicals. I must confess, however, that I am not an admirer of Lukacs' work—though, to be sure, the current practitioners of "Marxist" criticism do not begin to approach him.

and Trotsky in a way that makes Franklin look like a political primitive. The critics were writers like Harold Rosenberg, Philip Rahv, Lionel Trilling, Kenneth Burke, Edmund Wilson, and Irving Howe. All were anti-Stalinist, some were anti-communist as well. The point is that sensitivity to the political and historical dimensions of literature is not a monopoly of critics committed to revolutionary change— though, to be sure, those who are on different sides of the barricades will read the politics of the work or understand its historical significance in different ways. Franklin must account for the intense and intelligent political literary criticism of those who were neither communists nor New Critics in the thirties, forties, or fifties, if his view of modern criticism is to begin to have cogency.

What is curious about Franklin's performance is how much of it rests on his talent for creating a stereotype—and not so much of the discipline as of the person teaching the discipline. The essay begins with our professorial parasite in "a tie and a jacket" and ends with an optimistic counter stereotype of radical professors being culturally revolutionized and shedding their neckties. ("Professors of the world unite —you have nothing to lose but your neckties," would make a wonderful marching slogan.) We never get beyond the stereotypes to a view of what real people are doing and thinking in the profession.

A distinguished young critic, Frederick Crews, whose literary politics has recently taken a radical turn, acknowledges the fact that the interest in the political dimension of literary study is not the monopoly of the radical left. "It could be argued that the very best American discussion of literature was generated by the political ferment preceding World War II. Critics like Wilson, Trilling, Burke, Kazin, and Howe had to ask themselves where ideology ended and art began. Their urgently personal efforts to accommodate their sense of complexity to their politics, which seemed to be falling in ruins at the end of the thirties, yielded apprehensions of literature that were full of a clarifying passion. One need not agree with the accommodations themselves in order to grant the importance of the effort and the excitement it generated for others. When we compare such criticism with the formalism and static didacticism that have characterized much of the intervening period, we may wonder whether a certain political anguish may not be essential to good criticism." [3]

This is fine, yet Crews at the same time feels compelled (such is the spirit of the times) to make the ritualistic Marxist connection between the present stage of capitalism and the aesthetic or intellectual superstructure. "Recent criticism usually expresses the values of capitalism in its monopoly phase. Not justice and passion, but order and sophistication are implicitly treasured. The critic's relation to the text is manipulative rather than involved. Instead of accepting and examining the temperamental affinity to treat a certain author, he displays his capacity to perform correct and efficient operations that will give him total possession of the work. Writers who may have been scarcely able to contain their sensuality or savage indignation are thus transmuted into masters of cunning who have subliminally engineered our responses. Their seeming disunities are secret unities after all—indeed, are devices to trip us up. And if it is often hard for us to accept such a depiction of the writer, we at least know that the critic has succeeded in replacing *his* vulnerable feelings with cold and subtle strategy. It is like the computerized pacification of a province." [4] The "argument" is well-phrased but shoddy, unworthy of Crews's talents. It rides largely on the use of metaphor in which images like operations, devices, engineering, manipulation, strategy, and computerized pacification do the work of persuasion rather than demonstration. "Computerized pacification" is particularly gross, because it suggests without any argument that those engaged in the New Criticism share the mentality of those engaged in "pacifying" South Vietnam. The implication, if Crews is serious, is slanderous.

Moreover, the "total possession" of a work would more accurately define the Marxist's apprehension of a work of literature, rather than the new critic whose justification for addressing himself again and again to a work is a sense (real or simulated) of the work's inexhaustibility—and his "liberal" tolerance of a variety of approaches. I place the word liberal in quotation marks, because I do not mean to suggest a crude correlation between political and literary criticism, but I do want to show that this metaphorical game can be played to serve any ideological purpose.

Another radical critic playing this game, James Goldberg, connects Mark Schorer's interest in technique (in his famous essay "Technique as Discovery") with the repressive bureaucratic modalities of centralized government. Here is the pertinent passage from Schorer's essay: "Modern criticism, through its exacting scrutiny of literary texts, has demonstrated with finality that in art beauty and truth are indivisible and one. The Keatsian overtones of these terms are mitigated and an old dilemma solved if for beauty we substitute form and for truth content. We may, without risk of loss, narrow them even more, and speak of technique and subject matter. Modern criticism has shown us that to speak of content as such is not to speak of art at all, but of experience; and that it is only when we speak of the *achieved* content, the form of the work of art as a work of art, that we speak as critics . . . We are no longer able to regard as seriously intended criticism of poetry which does not assume these generalizations; but the case for fiction has not yet been established. The novel is still read as though its content has some value in itself, and as though technique were not a primary but a supplementary element, capable perhaps of not unattractive embellishments upon the surface of the subject, but hardly of its essence." [5] Goldberg comments that this exemplifies "the classic process of bureaucratization . . . means swallowing ends / form swallowing content, method as rationality / technique as discovery." He cites Mannheim in support: "the fundamental tendency of all bureaucratic thought is to turn all problems of politics into problems of administration." [6]

Schorer's slippery translations (from beauty and truth to form and subject matter, from truth to content to subject matter) are extremely vulnerable and his claim that New Criticism has achieved the status of exact knowledge even in dealing with poetry is presumptuous, but so are Goldberg's aggressive translations of Schorer's terms to the language of politics and administration. One of the worst things about contemporary literary education is the way it has sanctioned the replacement of argument based on logic and evidence by free (metaphorical) association, and the evidence for it can be found in the work of its radical critics. The mood of resentment toward established methods of criticism and scholarship simply causes radical critics to play false with the truth. Like Roszak, Franklin and Goldberg in crasser and more irresponsible ways deform the object of attack in order to serve their polemical purposes.

As for Crews's view that the subversive element in literature has been domesticated by recent critics, one can easily show that the process of domestication has always been an academic tendency, and that the subversive quality is not necessarily a matter of leftist politics. Among domesticated subversive writers can be found reactionaries like Swift, Nietzsche, and D. H. Lawrence. Domestication and distortion of literature is an old academic habit of critics and scholars of all political persuasions.

Indeed, the most significant effort to domesticate literature is the effort of modern criticism to come to terms with the scandalous attraction that major modern writers have felt toward reactionary ideas, in a number of cases fascism. Most critics, writing from democratic and liberal biases, find themselves embarrassed by the politics of writers whom they greatly admire and are unable or unwilling to confront the phenomenon. They have of course been assisted by an aesthetic doctrine that renders the politics irrelevant or subordinate to the art of the work. What this aesthetic does—as I have suggested in the previous chapter—is neutralize the political motives of the art and the criticism. Note the case is the opposite to what Crews suggests is the trouble. The attempt is to domesticate not the radical or revolutionary left but the reactionary element to benign liberal or democratic purposes.

Critics find themselves reduced to one of several strategies. They admit the reactionary, even fascistic character of the literature, but set it aside as irrelevant to what really matters—the aesthetic or "formal" character of the work— and then proceed to explain it away as something that is transformed or sublimated or attenuated in the realm of art. Politics is the soluble subject matter that dissolves and loses its identity in an aesthetic solution. (Thus the despotism of Don Ramon in Lawrence's *The Plumed Serpent* is seen as a function of the structure of relationships in the novel and not something that can be directly transferred to the political realm.) Lawrence, it is argued, recoiled from despotic fascism as an actual fact. The tacit assumption is often that no true artist would tolerate actual fascism, an assumption that breaks down in the presence of Pound and Pirandello, to name only two major instances. Or critics may consider the reactionary politics an important fact, insist that it be recognized, even condemn it, but leave it standing as an independent element of the work, somewhat unconnected with its aesthetic authority. Of course, if the critic is lucky enough to be reactionary himself, the reactionary politics will offer no problem at all—though he might have to protect his writer against the charge of fascism. Indeed, the reactionary politics will become part of the aesthetic authority of the work.

A radical critique of modern criticism might legitimately point out that all these approaches suffer from the habit of splitting up the politics and the art. When politics is considered as a separate element, the critic can do little more than approach it with the fixed categories of political discourse: he identifies this statement as liberal, that as conservative, another as reactionary. The effect is to see the politics as a merely adventitious element in the work—as if Yeats or Pound or Lawrence, given what they were as artists and persons, could have had any other kind of politics. But the political implication of a work is bound up with the imaginative disposition of the artist. His development as an artist, which includes matters of language, characterization, narrative method, may also be a matter of politics. The way he thinks about his characters, their pasts and their futures, may have political implications. (This is not to say that the politics may never be adventitious to the art.) Criticism too often takes the apolitical or antipolitical claims of literature on its own terms. Modern literature makes a kind of propaganda through its aestheticism (see Flaubert's *Sentimental Education* and Yeats's "Easter 1916") in diverting the reader from the claims of the political will or in attacking these claims.

The effect of splitting the art and the politics is to produce a peculiarly schizophrenic response to a work. One begins with a predetermined hostility to reactionary politics, for example; however, having learned the lesson about the need to suspend one's disbelief when confronted with art based on or containing alien assumptions, one finds oneself moved by the aristocratic feeling of a Yeats or a Nietzsche or possibly by the fascism of a Pound. The schizophrenia can be resolved either way, the most rewarding solution being the overcoming of the initial political hostility by a "suspension of disbelief." The other way is not rewarding because the labels one uses to characterize political positions have the effect of blurring or making opaque the experiential character of those positions. To say "reactionary" for a liberal or "radical" for a conservative is to disintegrate the liberal's attention to the living content of the reactionary position or the conservative's attention to the living content of the radical position. In other words, the New Critical insistence (derived from Coleridge) on suspending one's disbelief may be, paradoxically, a way of overcoming the impoverishing split in the reader's response to the political and aesthetic aspects of the work of art.

In a recent study of the reactionary content of modern literature, John R. Harrison betrays the limitations of a political attention to literature that is discontinuous with an aesthetic awareness of the literary process. What Harrison gives us is the obverse of the aesthetic habit of talking about the art separate from the politics. "Literature cannot be judged simply on what the writer says, but neither can it be judged satisfactorily if we ignore what the writer says. The writer's views may, as in the case of Yeats, help to work some wonderful transformation in technique; but the reader's enjoyment is almost certainly reduced by his antipathy to the *content* of what he is reading. It might also be argued that the writer's achievement is lessened." [7] Harrison's concession to the aesthetic side is wholly inadequate as his subsequent "practical criticism" of Yeats's performance bears out. Narrowing the aesthetic dimension to technique or seeing it, as he does later, as a matter of the sincerity of the poet's eloquence, he is wholly insensitive to the effect that the aesthetic of the work has on its political content—indeed, to the politics of the aesthetic act itself. Thus Harrison concedes the emotional power of Yeats's "reactionary" view of the traditional past.

Yeats' defense of the traditional past is quite beautifully expressed in *Coole Park and Ballylee, 1931*. The tone is one of calm, quiet acceptance and resignation. It is a personal tribute to a friend who had encouraged him, and to an estate which had sheltered and inspired him.

> "Upon the border of that Lake's a wood
> Now all dry sticks and a wintry sun,
> And in a copse of beeches there I stood."

Even if the reader thinks that privilege of birth and inherited wealth is wrong, he must be moved by such sincere and personal sentiment.

> We were the last romantics—chose for theme
> Traditional sanctity and loveliness;
> Whatever's written in what poet's name
> The book of the people; whatever most can bless
> The mind of man or elevate a rhyme;
> But all is changed, that high horse riderless,
> Though mounted in that saddle Homer rode.
> Where the swan drifts upon a darkening flood.[8]

Harrison cannot really account for the power of the poem to move us. All he does is assert its superiority to the work of "the communist poets of the 1930s" who lacked Yeats's "depth and understanding" of traditional values. Is the depth and understanding a matter of technique? It is hard to imagine what an affirmative answer would mean. Or is it a mark of the moral and spiritual authority of the voice of the poem? If so, how significant a judgment is the term "reactionary" even from a liberal and democratic point of view.

Any honest view of the political character of works of literature will have to account for the fact that during the last two centuries there exists an inverse relation between the aesthetic quality of a work of literature and radical politics —especially in works of art in which the political content is explicit and central. I have in mind the political novels of Flaubert, Conrad, Tolstoy, and Dostoevsky and the poetry of great modern poets like Yeats, Eliot, and Pound. There are to be sure exceptions: Rimbaud, Mayakovsky, certain surrealists. But it is a remarkable fact that the literary imagination since the French revolution has been more often than not skeptical or conservative or outrightly reactionary in relation to radical or revolutionary claims—in politics, if not in art. Of course, one can simply deny the value of these works (as Franklin is obviously prepared to do) and compose a syllabus of mediocre works that are "politically right" —a proletarian literature for which Franklin does not give a single instance. (Franklin's particular literary judgments scarcely encourage confidence in any proletarian literature he might advocate—see his judgments of Swift and Eliot above.) To do this is to replace "formalism and static didacticism," to use Crews's phrase, with static didacticism of another kind: revolutionary propaganda. I am not saying that "revolutionary" literature of high quality does not exist. I am arguing against the obverse of what Conor Cruse O'Brien calls counterrevolutionary subordination—that is, subordinating the integrity of an intellectual or imaginative discipline to political, albeit revolutionary, purposes. It is distressing that at this late date (after the experience of cultural Stalinism) the battle against the political vulgarization of the literary process has to be waged again.

And it must be waged not simply in the interest of aesthetic and intellectual freedom, but in the interest of the democratic experience itself. The relationship between high culture and the artistic imagination, on the one hand, and the radical democratic conscience, on the other, has always been tense and uneasy, yet it has profited both sides.

High Culture and Democracy

The embarrassments that culture has suffered in America are not simply the consequences of the peculiarities of American life. They reflect the tension between culture and democracy. "In aristocratic societies," Tocqueville remarks in *Democracy in America,* "the class that gives the tone to opinion and has the guidance of affairs, being permanently and hereditarily placed above the multitudes, naturally conceives a lofty idea of itself and man." [1] To anyone of democratic sensibility there is something offensive in the phrase "above the multitudes" and the easy assumption that a genuinely lofty attitude is the consequence of feeling above the majority. What is immediately offensive is the individuousness implied in the cultural idea—that the loftiness (what we call an appreciation of "the higher things") can be fostered and enjoyed only if others are felt to be below. The feeling of offense understandably produces a resentment against the cultural idea that one finds among democrats and radicals. If culture denies access to the multitudes it cannot be worth very much to man. (The feeling of invidiousness should be distinguished from the feeling against the multitudes—which is not necessarily antidemocratic. Those who oppose the tyranny of the majority may at the same time value each individual of the majority in his capacity as individual. What might be feared in the multitudes is coerciveness, the reduction of individual reason, imagination, and will to herd sentiment.)

It is impossible to deny that invidiousness has been characteristic of certain aesthetic and cultural arguments of the nineteenth century. If we turn to Renan, Flaubert, Baudelaire, Nietzsche, what we find is a strenuous insistence that only an elite can foster and enjoy the benefits of the cultural life. The insistence is sometimes so strenuous and ill-tempered that it would seem inextricably bound up with the idea of culture itself. Ernest Renan expresses this view with Darwinian ruthlessness. "It is necessary to affirm that we can hardly conceive of high culture prevailing in a portion of humanity without another portion serving it in a subordinate role. The essential thing is that high culture establish itself and render itself mistress of the world.* What is essential is less the creation of enlightened masses than the creation of geniuses and of an audience capable of understanding them. If the ignorance of the masses is a necessary condition for that, so much the worse. Nature does not stop before such concerns; she sacrifices entire species so that others find the essential conditions of their life." [2] We have apparently come a long way from the dream of the enlightenment, in which the political and cultural franchise would be extended to all of mankind. Of course, between the *philosophes* and Renan there loom the great events of the French Revolution. In their dream of a liberated mankind, the *philosophes* did not envisage a mass democracy. Renan's Darwinian ruthlessness is the vicious excess of a generally shared perception among literary men of the philistinism of bourgeois society. The contempt for the vulgar rich (a literary emotion) is extended to the proletarian "canaille" who are seen as motivated by the same mean material passion that motivated the successful bourgeoisie. (During the Paris Commune of 1871 the insurgent lower classes are viewed as ugly, mean-spirited, incompetent, envious, and worse.†)

* This view of the exploitative character of the cultural life seems to me more persuasive than the Marxist conception of superstructure. In the Marxist view, art is merely an expression of underlying economic interests. The view implied in Renan's statement is that cultural activity expresses its own interests. Like every other form of life, art has its own purposes, which it tries to make prevail.

† Paul Lidsky's *Les Ecrivains contre la commune* (Paris: Maspero, 1970) contains a veritable catalog of invective against the commu-

The aristocratic love of distinction turns the writer against the egalitarian and communal ambitions of the proletariat. The enthusiasm writers show for the revolution in 1789 is undermined as the revolution, periodically awakening from its dormancy, reveals its egalitarian and communal face in such episodes as the workers' revolt of June 1848 and the Paris Commune of 1871. The terror that often accompanies revolutionary justice is characteristically offered as an excuse, often honestly offered, for the disillusionment of writers (so it is in 1793, in 1848, and in 1871), but deeper than the fear of terror is the fear of the destruction of the cultural life that will occur in society as a result of the triumph of the masses.*

It is by no means clear that the cultural life depends on such ruthless invidiousness. But the belief in and love of distinction, of the heights, is essential to the cultural idea. Indeed, democratic resentment tends to confuse aristocratic arbitrariness with genuine difficulty of access. Alexander Herzen, a friend of the revolution, saw this with remarkable acuity. In Herzen's dialogue "Consolation" (included in *From the Other Shore*) the doctor shows the confusion to have existed in Robespierre, the inflexible logician of French revolutionary democracy. "Allow me, this is the second time

---

nard "canaille": "wild beasts," "stinking beasts," "vicious beasts" (Gauthier), "drunks, desperadoes" (Mendes), "madmen, savages" (Sands).

* In any event, the anti-communard writers were hardly entitled to their indignation about communard terror, since they were positively bloodthirsty in their dream of the revenge that the Versaillais would wreak upon the communards. Leconte de Lisle shared the sentiments of other writers when he expressed his keen anticipation of the return of the Versaillais: "Finally, it's over. I hope that the repression will be such that nothing will move any more, and for my part I wish it were extreme" (letter of May 29, 1871, to J—M de Heredia). Edmond Goncourt's satisfaction over the terrible repression is undisguised: "It is good. There has been neither conciliation nor negotiation. The solution has been brutal . . . It is twenty years of tranquility that the old society has before it if it dares do all that it can dare at this moment" (Journal, May 31, 1871, quoted in Lidsky, *Les Ecrivains contre la commune*, p. 76; my translation).

that you have called me aristocrat, which reminds me of
Robespierre's remark: 'L'atheisme est aristocrate.' If all Robespierre wanted to say was that atheism is open only to the
few, in the same way as the differential calculus or physics,
he would have been right, but when he said: 'atheism is aristocratic', he concluded from this that atheism is false. I
find this disgusting, this is demagogy, the submission of reason to an absurd majority vote. The inflexible logician of the
revolution faltered, and in declaring a *democratic* untruth
did not thereby restore popular religion, but only showed the
limits of his power." [3] All that one can expect from a democracy is the elimination of unearned privilege and mystification from the conditions of initiation.

Apart from the question of gift and talent, to which Herzen's doctor implicitly refers, there is also the matter of the
leisure to pursue the cultural life, a leisure Renan honestly
admits may demand the sacrifice of others. The aristocratic
character of culture is in part the necessary effect of a society of scarcity or of a society in which necessity is master.
As Tocqueville argues in *Democracy in America* the cultural life can scarcely be enjoyed in a society in which the
economic elite is obsessed with the pursuit of wealth or where
men are compelled by necessity to work eight or ten or
fourteen hours a day. In a society ruled by economic necessity
(as capitalist society of the nineteenth century was ruled by
necessity, the laws of which were spelled out by the dismal
science) the cultural life can be enjoyed only by those who
have the good fortune or the talent and will to exempt
themselves from economic necessity. Nor is it simply a matter
of enjoyment: "Not that in democracies the arts are incapable, in case of need, of producing wonders. This may occasionally be so if customers appear who are ready to pay for
time and trouble. In this rivalry of every kind of industry, in
the midst of immense competition and these countless experiments, some excellent workmen are formed who reach the
utmost limits of their craft. But they scarcely have an opportunity of showing what they can do; they are scrupulously

sparing of their powers; they remain in a state of accomplished mediocrity, which judges itself, and though well able to shoot beyond the mark before it, aims only at what it hits. In aristocracies, on the contrary, workmen always do all they can; and when they stop, it is because they have reached the limit of their art." [4]

I am not sure that aristocracy and democracy are the ultimate terms of the distinction. Tocqueville is here distinguishing between conditions of industrial life, for which democracy and aristocracy may be appropriate political terms at a certain stage in history. Given the vast market in a "democratic" society and the competition for markets among workmen, the cheapening of art is inevitable. But it is not at all clear that this is a necessary condition of democratic life. To be able to "reach the limit of one's art" one must be free of the economic necessity of compromising it. This is a necessary, if not sufficient, condition. And the democratization of leisure at least offers the opportunity for the extension of the cultural franchise, which is not envisaged by the foregoing distinction between aristocracy and democracy.

The adversary of culture is not necessarily democracy but the utilitarian regime of time, under which bourgeois and proletarian live. Even the proletarian who revolts against the bourgeois system is bound to the regime of time not only in his daily work but in his commitment to political activity. It is probable that his conception of culture will be of a crudely utilitarian order—that he will tend to find value only in what is useful to his political work. In the view of the aesthetic artist (a Flaubert, for instance) the utilitarian cultural and political ethic of the revolutionary is finally indistinguishable from the utilitarian ethic of bourgeois life. The identification of course is false in at least one fundamental respect: there is a world of difference between the bourgeois appetite for objects and proletarian need. Though it is true that an enriched proletariat cannot easily be distinguished from the middle class, the utilitarianism of the revolutionary after all is concerned (at least theoretically) with alleviating genuine need and suffering.

On the opposite side, the "disinterested" pursuits of the artist will appear to the revolutionary as another species of parasitism, not much different in moral quality from the bourgeois parasitism that sustains itself on the labor of others. Even Alexander Herzen holds this view—though in subtle form.

Who does not know the freshness of spirit created by carefree contentment? The poverty that produces a Gilbert is an exception. Poverty dreadfully warps the human soul, no less than wealth. Anxiety about mere material care crushes our capacities. But can well-being be within everyone's reach in the modern social order? Our civilization is a civilization of the minority—it is made possible only by the existence of a majority of proletarians. I am not a moralist, I am not sentimental: it seems to me that if in the past the minority really did lead agreeable lives and the majority remained silent, then this form of life was justified. I am not sorry for the twenty generations of Germans who were wasted in order to make Goethe possible, and am glad that the feudal dues of Pskov made it possible to rear Pushkin.

For aristocracy is really a more or less civilized form of cannibalism: a savage who eats his prisoner, a landowner who draws an enormous rent from his estate, a manufacturer who grows rich at the expense of his workmen, are mere varieties of the same cannibalism. And incidentally I am ready to defend cannibalism in its crudest form. If one man thinks of himself as a dish and another wants to eat him, let him eat him. They both deserve it; the one to be a man eater, the other to be his fodder.

So long as an educated minority, living off all previous generations, hardly guessed why life was so easy to live, so long as the majority, working day and night, did not quite realize why they received none of the fruits of their labour, both parties believed this to be the natural order of things, and the world of cannibalism could survive . . . but if once they realize that their truth is nonsense the game is up.[5]

It is to Herzen's credit that despite his sympathy for the revolution he acknowledges the pointlessness of moralizing about the social cost of art before revolutionary consciousness.* But it must be said that Herzen is still fundamentally in error.

That he must equate the artist with the landowner, manufacturer, and savage under the aspect of cannibalism is simply an instance of misplaced bad conscience. For one thing Herzen fails to acknowledge (here at least) what Goethe gives to society. Moreover, his instances of Goethe and Pushkin utterly ignore the reality of the lives of artists (Mozart, Schubert, Keats, Van Gogh, to name only a few) who lived in the most abysmal material circumstances and could be regarded as martyrs to their art. The real scandal is in the failure of society to support them.

The artist does not "enjoy" his "freedom from economic necessity" in any way resembling the capitalist's enjoyment of his profit or the aristocrat's pleasure in his leisure. Indeed, if a Keats or a Schubert is free of economic necessity, it is only that he has made a renunciation comparable to the renunciation of the monk, who pursues a purpose higher than material satisfaction. And in the great artists as in the great priests or for that matter the great revolutionaries the dedication to the higher purpose is daimonic. The fulfillment they seek entails suffering, feelings of inadequacy, humiliation—as well as the not very frequent moments of ecstatic consummation.

The enjoyment of the cultural heritage is to be sure a lesser activity: less arduous, less heroic. But if the enjoyment is genuine, it is active and strenuous, an attempt to reproduce in a lesser way the creative act itself. It is a mark of the philistine "apprehension" of the work of art that it simply expects music to wash over the ears, painting to represent the familiar pleasantly, literary work to communicate easily and transparently its meaning.

* Here he seems to be assuming an identity between the existence of revolutionary consciousness and what the masses actually think—though elsewhere he is keenly aware of the difference.

II

The connection between culture in its aristocratic aspect and democracy is that of tension rather than opposition. The tension is between the spirit of liberty or distinction and the ethos of equality. The French Revolution had mistakenly assumed that liberty and equality could be easily reconciled. The dilemma created by the rival claims of egalitarianism and aristocratic distinction is first suggested in the *Iliad*. Thersites is the archetypal spirit of mass democracy, condemning aristocratic distinction in the name of social justice. The gulf between the two modes of perception and feeling is illustrated by the violence of the encounter between Thersites and Odysseus in Book II. Thersites "screamed on alone, the endless talker. His mind was filled with many unruly words, with which to strive in rash disorder against kings—words which it seemed to him would raise a laugh among the Argives." Yet there is no denying Thersites' perception that "he who rules" has brought "the sons of the Achaeans to misfortune," or that the inferior Agammemnon has insulted the superior Achilles. But Thersites' hatred of the kings is so fundamental that it can only be perceived, even by the ordinary soldiers who have internalized the values of kings, as ludicrous resentment, of which the ugly bandy-legged Thersites is the appropriate physical incarnation. Thersites cannot make himself understood, so he must rail. Odysseus cannot "reason" with Thersites, since he is the irreconcilable enemy of the system, so he threatens him with a beating if he continues "to strive with kings." The history of Western consciousness is partly the moral and aesthetic enfranchisement of Thersites. In the enlightened modern consciousness, the conflict between Thersites and Odysseus has become, so to speak, a tension of valuable rival claims.

The opposition between high culture and democracy then is a false opposition. To the extent that culture is the legacy of an aristocratic civilization, it is the natural basis for a critique of industrial civilization and mass democracy. At its best, its most enlightened, it refuses to abandon itself to nostalgia and daydream. It exists in fruitful tension with democratic experience, critical not of democracy per se (which it regards as an irreversible and morally desirable historical process) but of certain tendencies that debase and even betray democracy. The deadliest enemy of culture is totalitarianism, which is the triumph of the philistine element in mass democracy, supported by the state and the police, and filled with active hatred of individuality and distinction. The raison d'être of the aristocratic code, which many modern artists have inherited, is in its stress on excellence and distinction, in its cult of self-fulfillment and personal intensity and in its profound need for beauty and grace and the spaciousness in which a graceful existence is possible. If this is inimical to the present reality of mass democracy, it does not diminish the value of the code to any adequate conception of the good life. Political piety on the left forbids any contemptuous reference to the people or the masses. But the genuine problems created by a mass society appear obliquely even in the perspectives formulated by radicals. Thus Theodore Roszak in *The Making of a Counter Culture* speaks of the need for making our lives as "big as possible, capable of embracing the vastness of those experiences which, though yielding no articulate, demonstrable propositions, nevertheless awake in us a sense of the world's majesty." [6] Of course, to make our lives as big as possible requires a vast space and a thinning of the population. Similarly, every plan for progressive education begins with the assumption of a small spacious community. Implied is an impulse to avoid the mass —not its needs but its presence. It is a symptom of political cant to identify the aesthetic or intellectual life with parasitism and exploitation.

Moreover, despite the defensiveness of a Renan or a Flaubert, culture has had the ambition to diffuse the benefits of its legacy to all classes of society. Matthew Arnold, the great English apostle of culture, sees this as the essential ambition of the cultural idea. Culture "seeks to do away with classes; to make the best that has been thought and known in the world current everywhere; to make all men live in an atmosphere of sweetness and light, where they may use ideas, as it uses them, freely—nourished and not bound by them. This is the social idea; and the men of culture are the true apostles of equality. The great men of culture are those who have had a passion for diffusing, for making prevail, for carrying from one end of society to the other, the best knowledge, the best ideas of their time; who have laboured to divest knowledge of all that was harsh, uncouth, difficult, abstract, professional, exclusive; to humanize it, to make efficient outside the clique of the cultivated and the learned, yet remaining the *best* knowledge and thought of the time, and a true source, therefore, of sweetness and light." [7] Culture (implicit in Arnold's view) is the religious idea of democracy. This is why the characterization of Arnold as an apostle is in a sense not metaphorical. Tocqueville testifies to the achievement of democracy in its capacity to diffuse the benefits of culture. "In free and enlightened democratic times there is nothing to separate men from one another or to retain them in their place; they risk or sink with extreme rapidity. All classes mingle together because they live so close together. They communicate and intermingle every day; they imitate and emulate one another. This suggests to the people many ideas, notions, and desires that they would never have entertained if the distinctions of rank had been fixed and society at rest. In such nations the servant never considers himself as an entire stranger to the pleasures and toils of his master, nor the poor man to those of the rich; the farmer tries to resemble the townsman, and the provinces to take after the metropolis. No one easily allows himself to be reduced to the mere material cares of life; and the humblest artisan casts at times an eager and a furtive glance into the higher regions of the intellect. People do not read with the same notions or in the same manner as they do in aristocratic communities, but the circle of readers is unceasingly expanded, till it includes all the people." [8] Democracy, ideally, is not only interested in a more equitable distribution of political power, it is also concerned to distribute the cultural wealth.

At moments of revolutionary struggle the conflict between artistic and cultural activity and political exigency is inevitable, and it is perhaps futile to moralize about the conflict. Artistic and intellectual activity in its insistence on following its own laws, its own inspiration, comes ineluctably to be regarded by the revolution as egoistic, parasitic, and destructive—though unlike the exploiter, the intellectual and the artist are creative and productive. Though it may be futile to moralize about it, there is a historical irony in the conflict. The cultural idea created by poets, artists, and men of letters of the eighteenth and nineteenth centuries, stripped of its aristocratic invidiousness, is in one sense the motive of the democratic revolution. The revolutionary dream is the realization of the Idea in history (in its rationalistic version) or the realization of the Dream of beauty (in its romantic version). Having triumphed over economic necessity men will enter their true estate of creative activity, intellectual meditation, noble conduct: they will achieve true freedom. Ironically (given the present animus against high culture), culture has been the inspiration of hubristic revolutionary ambitions, deserving the kind of critical scrutiny it has not received from its unwitting adversaries, a scrutiny I intend to give it in the next two chapters.

Utopia and the Irony of History

If the recent resurgence of utopian thinking has not transformed the world, it has significantly altered the sense of
political and cultural possibility—especially among the
young. The political immediacy of the issues, the intensity of
feeling that utopian claims provoke, and the current mistrust
of historical perspective as a reactionary blinder to present
possibility have intimidated and impoverished our understanding of the utopian idea. In this and the following chapter, I try to cut under the present level of argument by plac-
ing the subject in a historical perspective. Only a will to
delude oneself can argue for an insistence that we divest ourselves of whatever we might learn from that history.

Until the eighteenth century the task of the literary imagination was to understand the world, not to change it.
Thomas More never permitted himself the illusion that the
dream of a brave new world could transform the political
and social condition of man. Utopia was "nowhere" for
More. When William Morris in the nineteenth century wrote
News from Nowhere he was of course playing with More's
name for the ideal republic. Morris, unlike More, was fired
with a revolutionary belief that nowhere can become somewhere. Between More and Morris looms the Enlightenment,
which created a sense of possibility for radical political and
social change.

For More the realization of Utopia is precluded by his
Christian view of man's prideful nature. Toward the end of
the book, Raphael Hythloday, the man who brought the

good news of Utopia, remarks: "Pride, like a hellish serpent gliding through human hearts—or shall we say, like a sucking fish that clings to the ship of state?—is always dragging us back, and obstructing our progress towards a better way of life . . . this fault is too deeply ingrained in human nature to be easily eradicated." [1] Hythloday does not quite say that man's pridefulness is incorrigible, but his pessimism is very strong. Indeed, so confirmed is he in this feeling that in his view neither an appeal to enlightened self-interest nor the grace of God would have any power to effect Utopia. While More feels free to play with alternative political ideas, he could not seriously propose that the justice that inhered in his conception of an ideal polity gave anyone the authority to try to change the existing order.

The belief that utopia can be realized is sanctioned by two assumptions, which had authority in the Enlightenment: the assumption that natural man is good or at least not radically evil and the assumption that political authority originates or should originate in a rational arrangement among men—an arrangement expressed in a Social Contract. The two assumptions working together in Rousseau became a justification for altering the social order. The new faith in Reason was connected with the growing authority of science. The success of scientific theory in its account of the physical universe spurred the development of a moral science of man, which would be the basis for rational progress. Turgot and Condorcet are critical figures in the development of a philosophy of history in which moral ideas, based on science, become the motor force of historical development. For Turgot the dynamic agent of historical progress is Genius, the embodiment of these ideas. Turgot's conception achieved, as it were, its apotheosis in Hegel's postulation of the World Historical Individual, whose task it is at every stage of historical development to realize the Idea in history.

It is hardly surprising then that for those whose stake in the existing order was threatened, the very exercise of intellect, let alone the fact of new ideas, became suspect. The

Marchese del Dongo in Stendhal's *The Charterhouse of Parma* "professed a vigorous hatred of enlightenment: 'It is ideas, he used to say, that has ruined Italy.' " [2] The year is 1796, the French Revolution has already occurred, and the finger of blame is understandably pointed to the ascendancy of new ideas. The Marchese is merely expressing a sentiment widely shared by members of his class. "For the last half-century, as the *Encyclopedia* and Voltaire gained ground in France, the monks had been dinning into the ears of the good people of Milan that to learn to read, or for that matter to learn anything at all was a great waste of labour, and that by paying one's exact tithe to one's parish priest and faithfully reporting to him all one's little misdeeds, one was practically certain of having a good place in paradise." [3] In the aristocratic world of *The Charterhouse* Jacobinism and braininess tend to be associated. Political prudence in Parma consists of concealing one's intelligence, should one have the misfortune to possess any.

In the Marchese's aversion for ideas is the reductio ad absurdum of a formidable philosophical opposition to the utopianism of the Enlightenment. Tocqueville and Burke, the most distinguished exponents of the position, were to take the enthusiasm for ideas that marks the Enlightenment as the very source of its viciousness. In his classic study of *The Old Regime* Tocqueville characterizes the literary intellectuals of the Enlightenment in terms that scarcely conceal his contempt for them. "The sight of so many absurd and unjust privileges, whose evil effects were increasingly felt on every hand though their natural cause was less and less understood, urged, or rather, forced them towards a concept of natural equality of all men irrespective of social rank . . . Their way of living led these writers to indulge in abstract theories and generalizations regarding the nature of government, and to place a blind faith in those. For living as they did, quite out of touch with practical politics, they lacked the experience which might have tempered their enthusiasms . . . As a result our literary men became much bolder in

99

their speculations, more addicted to general ideas and systems, more contemptuous of the wisdom of the ages . . . In
the nation-wide debacle of freedom we had preserved one
form of it; we could indulge, almost without restriction, in
learned discussions of the origin of society, the nature of
government, and the essential rights of man." [4]

The inadequacy of Tocqueville's account is in its implicit
conservative assumption that a relatively fixed hierarchical
conception of the social order based on what he elsewhere
calls "the ancient laws of society" is incontestable wisdom.
For Tocqueville (as for Burke) the ancient laws of society
are rooted in the natural order of things. This natural order
involves a recognition of and acquiescence in the time-hon-
ored separations and invidious differences that exist among
the classes of society. In his *Recollections of 1848,* Tocqueville refers several times with contempt to the social ambitions of the servant class, who no longer accept their predes-
tined roles in society. He gives this contemptuous report of
his friend Blanqui's (not the revolutionary) overhearing of a
conversation among his servants during the June revolt:
"Next Sunday (it was Thursday then) *we* shall be eating the
wings of the chicken. Blanqui was very careful not to hear
these little monkeys . . . It was not until after the victory
that he ventured to send back the ambitious pair to their
hovels." [5] Implied in these sentences is the virtue of resigned
acceptance of one's social station. But resigned acceptance
can hardly be demanded or expected where hierarchical pre-
destination has been destroyed. Both the commercial and
democratic revolutions, as Tocqueville knew, had irreversi-
bly eliminated the feudal conception of social and economic
function. If society becomes open to everyone (*la carrière est
ouverte aux talents*—in Napoleon's famous sentence), then
one can no longer simply attribute the ambitions of the
lower classes to envy, the unmerited yearning for what another possesses. The moral advantage of the new social mo-
bility is that for the first time it makes possible—though it
by no means assures—an authentic accommodation between
one's capacities and one's social function.

In the *Recollections* Tocqueville sees the envy of the servant not simply as objectively immoral or criminal, but as a source of unhappiness for the servant. Of course, the happiness of the resigned servant is the presumption of the aristocrat. What Tocqueville (or any aristocrat) sees is the agreeable effect that the servant has on him. The aristocrat has no real perception of the conscious or unconscious price that the servant pays in denying himself for the ideals of service and deference. The vulnerability of Tocqueville's view can be vividly seen if we contrast it with a passage, already cited, from Alexander Herzen, Tocqueville's rival commentator on the events of 1848. "So long as an educated minority, living off all previous generations, hardly guessed why life was so easy to live, so long as the majority working day and night, did not quite realize why they received none of the fruits of their labor, both parties believed this to be the natural order of things, and the world of cannibalism could survive. People often take prejudice or habit for truth, and in that case feel no discomfort: but if once they realize that their truth is nonsense, the game is up. From then onwards it is only by force that a man can be compelled to do what he considers to be absurd. Try and organize fasts without faith. It is out of the question . . . Once the workers no longer want to work for another—that's the end of cannibalism, the point where aristocracy stops." [6]

Tocqueville is, of course, a complex figure, and I have here represented only one side of his complexity. It is sufficiently clear from *Democracy in America* (his master work) that his was a divided soul. On the one hand, he was attached to the old aristocratic order; on the other hand, he had an incisive and sympathetic understanding of the egalitarian ideal. Despite his aristocratic attachment, he had come to regard democracy not only as an irreversible historical process, but as a morally desirable one. His aristocratic biases became part of his remarkable capacity for criticizing the destructive tendencies of mass democracy, for seeing democracy in a perspective larger than mere enthusiasm for it. However deficient Tocqueville's critique may be, he has caught hold of a permanent truth about utopian thinking. Once in history, utopia becomes vulnerable to its pejorative sense, even for those who share the desire for a radical transformation of society.

I should pause here and say something about the way in which I am using the terms utopian and utopianism. There are at least two reasons why the terms are without precise, agreed-on definition in the scholarly and critical literature— that is, without the kind of definition that has been given to a conventional literary term like pastoral. One reason is that the utopian imagination is still in process and that its full reality has not exhausted itself, as I hope to show; another is that it is as much a political category as it is a literary category—and the term itself is a polemical issue. Those who use the term utopian in a pejorative sense will tend to see its putative "unreality" as part of the definition of the term, whereas utopians or utopists (to distinguish them from the inhabitants of More's imaginary society) will see utopia in platonic terms as the substantial world in the light of which our own world becomes enigmatically unreal. From the utopian point of view, it is puzzling that people can live as they do.

I would hope that my sense of the utopian emerges contextually from my argument, but I should indicate certain of its features. Utopianism in my present usage is the imagination of an ideal political and social order based on moral reason. In such an order justice prevails and men are reasonably happy. No such imagination can ever be absolutely discontinuous with existing historical conditions. More's utopia is not only a response to existing evils in late fifteenth and early sixteenth century England, his solutions are inevitably shaped by those conditions. In comparison with utopian economies conceived after the Industrial Revolution (for example, the utopian economy of Bellamy's *Looking Backward*) the economy of More's Utopia is a relatively spartan one (though needs are satisfied and utopians have their share of comforts). The equitable distribution of the goods of life and the communal ethic sanctioned by a belief that God is present in the natural world resembles somewhat the economy and society of an ideal medieval monastery. For moral reasons, More may have preferred a relatively spartan economy as less corrupting to the character, but these moral reasons are themselves in part at least a product of the world in which More lived. Yet the historical conditioning of the imagination of utopia should not obscure what I take to be a fundamental feature of utopian thinking. Unlike ideology, which rationalizes an existing state of affairs or a power motive, utopia is, so to speak, disinterested. Utopianism begins with an idea and tries to exfoliate it according to the standards of moral reason in an uncompromising and intransigent way. Political realism, as it is understood in the practical political world, is alien to the utopian mind. This is no problem so long as utopia remains a *jeu d'esprit* or an oblique form of satire or even a source for practical ideas for reform. Indeed, insofar as utopianism expresses the view that the present limitations of social and personal life are not ultimate and are subject to rational change, it can be a liberating view—utopia's permanent contribution to the political and social life. This explains my concern to point out the inadequacy of Tocqueville's conservative critique of Enlightenment utopianism. However, utopianism becomes problematic, indeed pernicious, when it enters the historical realm with ambitions to transform the political and social order according to an idea.

The problem resides in the mediations that occur between idea and event, between intention and historical process. Indeed, the failure of utopian thinkers to appreciate the mysteries of mediation is the object not only of a conservative critique, but of a Marxian criticism as well. The relationship between Marx and utopianism is an ambiguous, difficult, and extremely important chapter in the history of modern utopianism. In *Socialism: Scientific and Utopian,* Engels clearly distinguishes the Marxian enterprise from utopianism: "The solution of the social problems, which as yet lay hidden in the undeveloped economic conditions, the Utopians attempted to evolve out of the human brain. Society presented nothing but wrongs; to remove these was the task of reason. It was necessary, then, to discover a new and more perfect system of social order and to impose this upon society from without by propaganda, and wherever it was possible, by the example of modern experiments. These new social systems were foredoomed as utopian [note the pejorative use of the word here]; the more completely they were worked out in detail the more they could not avoid drifting off into pure fantasies." And Engels puts the utopians in an adversary ideological role when he notes that "the kingdom of reason [is] nothing more than the idealized kingdom of the bourgeoisie." [7]

This is not to deny the inspirational force of utopian ideas. Engels himself qualifies the severe criticism he directs against utopian thinkers when he speaks of his "delight in the stupendously grand thoughts and germs of thought that everywhere break out through their fantastic covering, and to which those Philistines are blind." [8] Marx and Engels would be the last to deny the power of ideas to change the world, but what they sought to develop was a science that mediates idea and the historical process, that makes the historical process the natural expression of the idea. Marx and Engels have this in common with the Burkean view: the dynamism of the political system is in the historical process (Burke would call it the tradition) and not in the presumptions of the abstract intelligence. The function of the intellect is to discover and join itself to the principle that moves and (for Burke) stabilizes political society. Of course, Marx's conception of the dynamic principle is radically opposed to the Burkean conception. For Marx, the dynamic principle is dialectical, disruptive, revolutionary, whereas for Burke it is "a condition of unchangeable constancy, [moving] on through the varied tenour of perpetual decay, fall, renovation and progression." [9] I have brought Marx and Burke together here (an odd couple) to stress Marx's affinity with the tradition of anti-utopian criticism. In the light of the historical failures of Marxism, scientifically and morally,* it has become customary to dismiss Marx's enterprise as utopian, often without an attempt to specify the way or ways his thought can be so characterized.

In my view, Marx's thought possesses a significant utopian element, but it would be false to the complexity of Marx's work to make a facile appropriation of it to the utopian tradition. This is usually the temptation of those who want to undercut Marx's claim to scientific status. Apart from the question of whether Marx was a scientist or not, he is unquestionably separated from the utopian tradition by his continuous awareness of what both Marx and Engels called "the irony of history." The classic narrative in the Marxian canon for this awareness is *The Eighteenth Brumaire of Louis Napoleon,* a text I would like to consider at some length. "Men make their own history, but they do not make it just as they please; they do not make it under circumstances chosen by themselves, but under circumstances directly encountered, given and transmitted from the past. The tradition of all the dead generations weighs like a nightmare on the brain of the living. And just when they seem engaged in revolutionizing themselves and things, in creating something that has never yet existed, precisely in such periods of revolutionary crisis they anxiously conjure up the spirits of the past to their service and borrow from them names, battle cries and costumes in order to present the new scene of world history in this time-honoured guise and this borrowed language. Thus Luther donned the mask of the Apostle Paul, the Revolution of 1789 to 1814 draped itself alternately as the Roman republic and the Roman empire, and the Revolution of 1848 knew nothing better to do than to parody, now 1789, now the revolutionary tradition of 1793 to 1795." [10]

* The phrase "the scientific and moral failures of Marxism" (for example, Stalinism) does not mean to imply that Marxism is a failure, an absurd notion to assign to so seminal and so potent a tradition of thought and action.

The phrase "time-honoured disguise and borrowed language" suggests a Machiavellian operation, and the very presence of Louis Napoleon on center stage is enough to authenticate the suggestion. Here is a typical characterization of Louis Napoleon's Machiavellianism: "An old crafty *roué,* he conceives the historical life of the nations and their performances of state as comedy in the most vulgar sense, as a masquerade where the grand costumes, words and postures merely serve to mask the pettiest knavery." [11]

But Marx's narrative in *The Eighteenth Brumaire* suggests something deeper and more interesting in the matter of deception and self-deception. Possessed by inherited ideas and images, historical actors, often with conscious sincerity, mask the objective aims of the historical process and find themselves or others find them the unwitting agents of unintended purposes. The irony of history results from man's incapacity for anticipating the historical process. In the case of the bourgeoisie, the self-deception is necessary and useful, because "unheroic as bourgeois society is, it nevertheless took heroism, sacrifice, terror, civil war and battles of peoples to bring it into being." [12] The bourgeois class had to conceal from itself the narrow bourgeois substance of its struggles in order to keep its enthusiasm on the high plane of "the great historical tragedy." The Roman costumes and phrases have the additional virtue of deceiving the proletariat, the potential irreconcilable antagonist of the bourgeoisie. The emerging proletariat enters into an alliance with the bourgeois revolution in its early stages because the bourgeoisie in its heroic universalist posture successfully deludes the proletariat into believing that it stands for the liberation of all mankind. In Marx's view the self-deceptions of the proletariat are a matter of ignorance that can be overcome, not of bad faith as they are in the case of the bourgeoisie. It is precisely the role of Marx, the master ironist in the service of the historical process itself, to unmask these deceptions so that the proletariat can know its true interests. (The proletariat does not require self-deluding illusions because its true aim is the heroic liberation of the majority of society.)

According to Marx, what the revolution of 1848 and its Bonapartist conclusion revealed, despite the illusory and farcical oppositions between different sections of the bourgeois class (the proletariat had been deluded into siding with the petit bourgeoisie in 1848) was the essential historical reality of the nineteenth century: the absolute hostility of the bourgeoisie to the real interests of the proletariat. The revealed unity of the bourgeoisie against the proletariat paradoxically was the basis for the eventual victory of the proletariat. In trying to take power in June 1848 (prematurely from the point of view of its capacity) the proletariat in effect united the bourgeoisie against itself and exposed the despotic character of the bourgeois republic when menaced. The illusions and myths by which the bourgeoisie tries to sustain itself in power were stripped away. Thus what the proletariat won in defeat was "the terrain for the fight for its emancipation, but by no means the emancipation itself." [13] That was to occur in the future. Marx puts it this way in *The Class Struggles in France: 1848–50:* "In a word, the revolution made progress, forged ahead, not by its immediate tragicomic achievements, but, on the contrary, by the creation of an opponent in combat with whom, only, the party of revolt ripened into a really revolutionary party." [14] With the advent of the proletariat, there is for the first time the possibility (or is it the inevitability?) of a revolution without myths or costumes—a revolution enacted with the full consciousness of what is being achieved. As Harold Rosenberg has put it: "committed to 'the sober reality' the proletarians would have to undergo without relief *the pathos of the historical.*" [15]

One cannot simply make a society from an idea in the brain; such an idea may indeed supply energy for the impulse to remake society, but the outcome, the forms of society that will result, will always depend on historical conditions that for various reasons cannot be anticipated. Here Marx is clearly opposed to utopianism. It would seem however that there is one large exemption from the irony of history in Marx's view—that is, the eventual revolutionary action of the proletariat. There are to be sure ironies in the career of the proletariat, which Marx and Engels remark with characteristic acuity—for instance, during the Paris Commune of 1871, "the irony of history" willed that the Blanquists and the Proudhonists do the opposite of what the doctrines of their schools prescribed, which Engels notes is usual when "doctrinaires come to the helm." [16] But the irony is provisional. The proletariat will see its interests in historical struggle, will discover in the historical process the idea that it will enact, the idea of a new society that it can realize through revolution. The proletariat will triumph and accomplish its purposes.

In a suggestive essay on *The Eighteenth Brumaire,* Harold Rosenberg is critical of Marx's attempt "to outline in advance the act that was to follow" since no one can predict whether the hero will have available to himself the potency "to perform the deed demanded by his time." [17] Moreover, what of the deed demanded by the time? How is that determined, who determines it? The proletariat expressing its will, its desire, in a spontaneously unanimous or even majoritarian way? Or is the deed not rather defined by the man of prophetic "scientific genius" supported by the revolutionary vanguard? As Lenin was subsequently to acknowledge, the revolutionary vanguard is the self-elected mind of the proletariat from which both the understanding of problems and their solutions emanate. It is not hard to see how the Marxian sense of the solution and of the moment for its imposition might resemble the rationalistic arbitrariness that Engels perceived in the approach of the utopian socialists.

By exempting the proletariat from the irony of history, Marx had placed himself in the company of his utopian rivals. Beyond the question of whether the proletariat has the potency and will to accomplish its purposes, there is also the matter of the nature of those purposes. Let us say that the proletariat does undergo the pathos of the historical in the cold light of sober reality. Does that necessarily assure the liberation of mankind, which is the goal of the historical process, the free development of each, which Marx saw as a condition for the free development of all? Marx's work does not provide an answer as far as I can make out, because his conception of the irony of history is confined to the disparities that exist between intention (real or declared) and historical outcome or consequence. The question of purposes, of what the consequences of the fulfillment of purposes would be, is not a real question for him. To be sure, he assumes that the triumph of the proletariat, its ownership of the means of production, the redistribution of social wealth, and the transformation of the social order into a classless society will eliminate the material and spiritual misery of the world, but he does not envisage the possibility of another kind of irony of history: the failure of the accomplished purpose to satisfy or, worse, the experience of the accomplished purpose as a kind of tyranny. Marx is constrained from doing so by virtue of his view of the historical process as the supreme court of appeal. It would simply be an exercise in futility for him if, doubting the benevolence of the purposes of the historical process, he imagined alternatives to them. Indeed, to imagine such alternatives would be from Marx's point of view a utopian act.

But would Marx have accepted this constraint without a belief in the benevolence of the historical process? What seems like an a priori belief in its benevolence is nicely illustrated by a passage from Alexander Herzen, who though not a Marxist writes here very much in a Marxian spirit: "'To accuse socialism of not having sufficiently elaborated its opinions nor developed its teaching, and of wanting nevertheless to realize them is an injustice. Social revolutions are never made before the battle, they begin by the negation of what is obsolete. The battle is a putting into practice of abstract social ideas . . . Utopias alone are elaborated and entirely prepared in advance: the Republic of Plato, the Atlantis of Bacon, the celestial realm of the Christians. The church was not all prepared in the Gospels, it developed in time, through struggle." [18] Both Herzen and Marx were confident that the condition of historical struggle would ultimately not betray "the abstract social ideas," though one might expect ironic peripeties on their path to concrete realization. There is no suspicion in the passage above of the possibility of an Orwellian denouement to the historical struggle. This is because the very idea of history in the work of men like Herzen and Marx is unalterably affected by the utopian legacy of Enlightenment thought. The idea of history as progress, whether in its linear or dialectical form, is in part an invention of the brain, subject itself to the irony of "real history." Marx and Engels deliberately refrained from blueprinting the future communist society, for that would be utopian fantasizing; yet their projection of a structured, benevolent movement of history into the future expresses the same utopian impulse they criticized. In effect Marx provides utopianism with its most persuasive historical rationale —in Marxian terms, with a real scientific basis. In the act of denying utopianism, Marx turns utopianism into a potent force in modern history, without however, solving its problems.

II

Modern antiutopianism is based on a perception of the tyranny of the idea. In *The Sentimental Education* (published in 1869) Flaubert had already dramatized the tyranny of utopian logic in the character of Senecal, the revolutionist nourished on the ideas of Rousseau, Saint-Simon, Fourier, Louis Blanc, and others. Senecal is the disinterested devotee of the Idea, who defends all attacks upon it "with the logic of a geometrician and the zeal of an Inquisitor." Modeling himself on Blanqui, who in turn modeled himself on Robespierre, Senecal enacts the authoritarian logic of his position by appearing in the wake of the Bonapartist coup d'etat as a police officer in the ranks of the forces of Order. We are prepared for this outcome by a speech given earlier by Senecal himself, when he "inveighs against the masses for their inadequacy." "Robespierre, by upholding the right of the minority had brought Louis XVI to acknowledge the National

Convention, and saved the people. Things were rendered legitimate by the end toward which they were directed. A dictatorship is sometimes indispensable. Long live tyranny, provided that the tyrant promotes the general welfare." [19]

The antiutopian critique, which Flaubert anticipates here, does not simply reject utopian ideas, which it regards as pernicious. It sees the utopian activity itself as pernicious. The paradox of utopianism from the antiutopian view is this. The utopian idea represents an impulse toward liberation, toward the personal and social fulfillment of man. However, when it gets incorporated into the historical process, it begins to exercise a constraint or tyranny of its own. Revolutionaries who deny the view of historical reality as complex, refractory to reason and will, and who insist on the power of the idea to transform the world often find themselves slaves to the idea—in the name, for instance, of historical necessity. Hannah Arendt makes this suggestive remark about the makers of the French Revolution: "There is some grandiose ludicrousness in the spectacle of these men—who dared to defy all powers that be and to challenge all authorities on earth, whose courage was beyond the shadow of a doubt—submitting, often from one day to the other, humbly and without so much as a cry of outrage, to the call of historical necessity, no matter how foolish and incongruous the outward appearance of this necessity must have appeared to them." [20] Miss Arendt calls them "the fools of history."

Fools perhaps, but in the circumstances it is by no means an easy matter to become wise. In an idea precipitated into the historical sphere there is a necessary logic that one cannot abandon at will—that one cannot abandon without abandoning the idea itself and a belief in its possible success in history. If one fails to understand this, one cannot possibly imagine the predicament of revolutionaries who have been purged in the putative interests of the revolution itself. The success with which many of them are persuaded to comply with their executioners even to the point of self-condemnation is a function of the extent to which the idea (historical reason, the dialectics of history) becomes part of the revolutionary conscience. The tyranny of the idea also occurs on lower levels of self-condemnation, where execution is not the conclusion. How difficult it is even for the most intelligent and experienced revolutionaries to see that the successful incarnation of the revolution has betrayed the revolution or worse that the revolution itself may be the tyrant. (Concerning the latter possibility, it is remarkable, for example, how despite Victor Serge's corrosive sense of the unfolding of the Russian Revolution in *The Case of Comrade Tulayev,* there is no contemplation of the possibility that this is the way *the* revolution unfolds. The true revolution remains outside the province of criticism.)

The tyranny of the idea is not like the tyranny of something recognizably evil, which merely threatens force. It is a seductive tyranny because it is the expression of the highest ideals of men: justice, self-fulfillment, communal harmony. Having claimed these ideals for its particular jurisdiction, utopia deprives men who continue to be mysteriously unhappy under its regime (a regime which may have its place in the mind as well as on a particular territory) of an alternative vision and consequently even of the power to say no to utopia. The tyranny of evil, of course, has no such power. How difficult, if not impossible, to say no to the very idea of happiness.

This is the essential basis of the antiutopian vision, which utopian rationalists of the liberal and revolutionary variety fail to grasp. Despite his intelligent and sympathetic efforts to come to terms with antiutopianism, George Kateb in his book *Utopia and Its Enemies* cannot escape the liberal feeling that at bottom there is something perverse, immoral, and ruthless in the antiutopian position that must simply be repudiated. His characterization of a principal source of antiutopian argument and sentiment, Dostoevsky's *Notes from the Underground* and its companion tale "The Dream of a Ridiculous Man," is revealing. In connection with these tales he asks us to keep in mind the man in the Myth of Er (which concludes Plato's *Republic*) "who had behaved well because he lived in a society with good regulations and chose for his next life the life of a tyrant, as if to show that deep down inside himself the beast remained all the time yearning for release, and never getting it, thanks only to the power of social constraint." Kateb goes on to say: "We can keep in mind Dostoyevsky's Underground Man who will go beserk (with Dostoyevsky's approval) just to upset the established harmony; and Dostoyevsky's Ridiculous Fellow who cannot avoid corrupting the utopia of his dream . . . It would seem that men itch to smash, especially to smash the perfect; to put it as generously as it can be put, they crave excitement, especially forbidden excitement; they cannot be tamed." [21]

This is not in the least generous; it is entirely an external and unsympathetic view of the underground man's claim—the view of the utopian rationalist whom the underground man is attacking. To be sure, the underground man makes the most unreasonable argument imaginable in opposition to rationality. "A man, always and everywhere, prefers to act in the way he feels like acting and not in the way his reason and interest tell him, for it is very possible for a man to feel like acting against his interests and, in some instances, I say that he *positively* wants to act that way—but that's my personal opinion. So one's own free, unrestrained choice, one's whim, be it the wildest, one's own fancy, sometimes worked up to a frenzy—that is the most advantageous advantage that cannot be fitted into any table or scale and that causes every system and every theory to crumble into dust on contact." [22] The complaint is directed against the laws of nature, which specify that a man always pursues his interest, his interest being defined as the pursuit of pleasure and the avoidance of pain. On the face of it, this utilitarian psychology is a perfectly reasonable psychology. Any humane society, it would seem, would foster and support it. More's utopians, we should recall, take the hedonistic view, which includes "the instinct to be reasonable in our likes and dislikes." "The Utopians . . . regard the enjoyment of life—

that is, pleasure—as the natural object of all human efforts, and natural, as they define it, is synonymous with virtuous living." [23]

What is at the root of the underground man's complaint is not the wild beast but the sentiment of a violated humanity. The underground man is protesting against the constraint of reason, of the idea that, to the extent that it rules men's minds, impoverishes them. Denied in the utopian view are the passions, in which there is an admixture of pain and suffering, which nonetheless—and utopian rationalists regard this simply as perversity—contribute to the sentiment of one's being, of one's particular humanity. It is reason that has secreted the poison that has made the underground man monstrous. At the end of the tale he fully reveals what has been implicit: that the laws of nature, the arithmetic that makes two times two four, the stone walls that circumscribe human existence, mere expressions of human reason, have denied the full flesh and blood reality of human beings—that he, like everybody else is only a creature of the idea. "I have only in my life carried to an extreme what you have not dared to carry halfway, and what's more you have taken your cowardice for good sense, and have found comfort in deceiving yourselves. So that, perhaps, after all, there is more life in me than in you. Look into it more carefully! Why, we don't even know what living means now, what it is, and what it is called! Leave us alone without books and we shall be lost and in confusion at once. We shall not know what to join, what to cling to, what to love and what to hate, what to respect and what to despise. We are oppressed at being men —men with a real individual body and blood, we are ashamed of it, we think it a disgrace and try to contrive to be some sort of impossible generalized man. We are still-born, and for generations past have been begotten, not by living fathers, and that suits us better and better. We are developing a taste for it. Soon we shall contrive to be born somehow from an idea. But enough." [24] The impression that remains of the underground man is not that he is an untamed beast gone beserk, but that he is the incarnation of reason gone beserk—a paradoxicalist who lives so completely in the mind that he is incapable either of having a true feeling or of recognizing one—it is never absolutely clear—except perhaps the feeling of energetic misery that pervades the tale.

The underground man is asserting the claim of freedom and the fullness of personal life (which, of course, he himself does not incarnate) against the constraining power of reason. The ultimate terms of conflict in Dostoevsky are freedom versus happiness or contentment. In the Grand Inquisitor chapter of *The Brothers Karamazov* the argument for freedom is sanctioned by Christ, who has returned to confront the pharisaism of his own church, whereas the idea of contentment is associated with the "benevolent" authoritarianism of the Grand Inquisitor. Christ answers the underground man's implicit yearning for a positive spiritual freedom. Though representing different stages in Dostoevsky's imaginative career, *Notes from the Underground* and the episode of the Grand Inquisitor are both antiutopian in their repudiation of the possibility of redemption through secular rationality.

Eugene Zamiatin's *We* (1920), perhaps the most distinguished of the antiutopian novels, recalls Dostoevsky both in substance and in manner. R-13 instructs the novel's hero in the myth upon which the state is founded in a manner resembling Ivan's relating of his dream of the Grand Inquisitor. "You see, it is the ancient legend of paradise . . . There were two in paradise and the choice was offered to them: happiness without freedom, or freedom without happiness . . . They fools that they were chose freedom. Naturally, for centuries afterward they longed for fetters, for the fetters of yore . . . No, listen, follow me! The ancient god and we . . . Yes, we helped god to defeat the devil definitely and finally. It was he, the devil who led people to transgression, to taste precious freedom . . . Done with Him! Paradise again! No more meddling with good and evil and all that . . . The

Well-Doer, the Machine, the Cube, the giant Gas Bell, the Guardians—all these are good. All this is magnificent, beautiful, noble, lofty, crystalline, pure. For all this preserves our non-freedom, that is, our happiness . . . Well, in short, these are the highlights of my little paradise poem." [25] The cheerful manner is inauthentic. For R-13, like the hero, knows the temptations of freedom. The tale belies the presumption of the myth that the very need for freedom has been overcome, that no price has been paid for happiness. (It is interesting to note in this connection the affinity between the spiritual authority of the church in its inquisitorial function and the role of utopia when it is experienced as oppressive by its citizens.)

The resistance to utopian tyranny takes the form of erotic passion, criminality, and suffering itself. In *We* the conversion of men to mathematical symbols cannot alone accomplish the purposes of control. The Well-Doer must resort to lobotomizing his subjects in order to assure their happiness. And though the novel concludes with the declaration that "reason will prevail," it continually bears witness to the ungovernable explosive energy of the universe. The Well-Doer has achieved a condition of entropy that is only temporary.

The principal drama is the hero's struggle against his love for the woman, whose name is I-330, because he "knows" that "love [in the Utopian definition] is a function of death." In language recalling *Notes from the Underground,* the hero nevertheless finds himself drawn to his beloved, longing even for the pain of distance that inevitably separates her from him. "How absurd to desire pain! Who is ignorant of the simple fact that pains are negative items that reduce the sum total we call happiness? Consequently . . . Well, no 'consequently' . . . Emptiness . . . Nakedness!" [26] The success with which utopia has been able to internalize the constraint of reason can be seen in the strangled expression of the hero, who can hardly complete his sentences—as if the impulses of revolt are trying to find a language against the mathematic coherence of the language of the state.

In Zamiatin's view, the revival of revolutionary impulse, difficult as it may be, is required to restore vitality to the world. The requirement is instinctively felt in the very physiology of men, though men need courage to act upon it. Zamiatin paradoxically opposes revolutionary instinct to utopian reason. "No revolution, no heresy is comfortable and easy. Because it is a leap, it is a rupture of the smooth evolutionary curve, and a rupture is a wound, a pain. But it is a necessary wound: most people suffer from hereditary sleeping sickness, and those who are sick with this ailment (entropy) must not be allowed to sleep, or they will go their last sleep, the sleep of death." [27] The full force of Zamiatin's paradoxical use of revolution can be grasped only when one keeps in mind the fact that Zamiatin was one of the early dissident Soviet writers, whose work from the orthodox revolutionary point of view is unquestionably counterrevolutionary.

George Orwell's *1984,* which shows the influences of *We,* dramatizes the despotic use to which reason is put when it ceases to be responsible to external reality and to common sense. The shibboleths "War is Peace," "Freedom is Slavery," "Ignorance is Strength" become possible statements because any experience, any fact, that denies these postulates are vaporized out of existence. Orwell, I think, is not fully alert to the implications of this in the formulation "freedom is slavery." Subject and predicate should have been reversed,* for the power of utopian reason is precisely in its capacity to convert the experience of slavery into the idea of freedom. For those who cannot accept the conversion, terror or disappearance is the only conclusion. Reason in its abstraction from reality comes to replace reality. O'Brien, the Inner Party Intellectual, instructs Winston in the nature of utopian reality. "Reality is not external. Reality exists in the human mind, and nowhere else. Not in the individual mind, which can make mistakes, and in any case soon perishes:

---

* Orwell does subsequently reverse the statement to make, in my view, a not very lucid point about slavery as the via media to immortality through the collective life of the party.

only in the mind of the Party, which is collective and im-
mortal." [28] The system develops a logic of its own, adjustments in the system concern the mutual relations of statements to one another. What began as an effort in the
Enlightenment to demystify the sanctions for political sover-
eignty becomes a powerful instrument of mystification in the
name of historical reason.

The antiutopian view is based less on empirical observation than on a perception of the unfolding of the logic of
utopia—hence its futurism. When it presumes to be a reading of the actual history of the past two hundred years, it
suffers from the abstractness that it decries in its utopian adversaries. In *After Utopia* Judith Shklar justly remarks that
antiutopian critics like J. L. Talmon and Michael Polanyi
(whom she calls conservative liberals) assume "a logic inherent in history" and consequently a rationalism they would
deprecate in others, when, for instance, Talmon tries to
make the case that Rousseau's "general will" is at the root of
modern totalitarianism.[29] In such a view, the real se-
quences of events in various countries are ignored. The reading of history, from the antiutopian view, must be substanti-
ated by a sociology of ideas, which the conservative liberals
for the most part fail to employ. There is doubtless an overly
strong tendentiousness in their work.

But it would be misleading to say that there is no historical evidence for the tyranny of utopian logic. I have already
cited political terror committed in the name of historical reason. And the self-coercive effect of utopian reason on those
who are devoted to the project of social transformation and
self-transformation is a historical reality. Our faith in technological reason as a source of liberation, which has been se-
verely jolted (and for good reason) in recent years, was in
large part sustained by a utopian confidence in its liberating
power. The fact that B. F. Skinner and others can still entertain the fantasy of creating a moral and rational environment
through the systematic conditioning of human beings means
that the utopian temptation remains very real. Though one

can never predict the actual role of ideas in history (assuming that we have learned the lesson about the irony of history), the failure to pursue the logic of an idea as it might be enacted in history involves the abdication of the responsibility of the intellectual in his role as teller of cautionary tales. The antiutopian view has been persuasive in its perception of the overweening faith in the world-transforming power and benevolence of reason, a faith that derives much of its supporting strength from the corollary belief that there is a historical plot through which reason works out its destiny.

In any event there has been in the twentieth century a general breakdown—though by no means a complete one— of utopian faith in "the intelligible plot of history presumed by various philosophies." For twentieth century philosophy, reason has either disappeared from history or manifested itself as horror. Of course, in the nineteenth century men like Tolstoy, Nietzsche, and Kierkegaard already assault the great hypostatization of historical reason from different perspectives. The testimony of modern literature, as we all know, is strong on the treachery and terrors of history. Thus Eliot in "Gerontion":

> Think now
> History has many cunning passages, contrived corridors
> And issues, deceives us with whispering ambitions
> Guides us by vanities. Think now
> She gives when our attention is distracted
> And what she gives, gives with such confusion
> That the giving famishes the craving.[30]

For Stephen (in *Ulysses*) history is a nightmare from which he is trying to awake.

The disintegration of the historical plot (of the belief in historical reason) is at once an occasion for despair and for hope. For those who are attached to the faith, in future progress implied by the plot the loss of faith is cause for despair; for those who have experienced the tyrannical constraints of historical necessity, there is something liberating in its disintegration. The contemporary revolutionary (if I can be so bold as to characterize him generically) has managed to be in a precariously equivocal position between belief and disbelief in the plot. He stands before a future undetermined by a historical ideology (unsanctioned by historical reason), open to the impositions of his will. Without the authority of ideology, of the plot, the sanctions of the new revolutionary spirit are (1) the moral power on its side and (2) the political power it feels it has to impose itself on events. But this confidence in the revolutionary will to impose itself on history would not be possible, it seems to me, if it were not for a strong vestigial belief in the benevolent mechanism of the historical plot. The openness that the contemporary revolutionary shows before the present and the future closes quickly on two unexamined assumptions: (1) that the present is worse than any future that the revolution might create, and (2) that the self-betrayals of past revolutions will be obviated by a willed refusal to repeat the past—to be achieved, for instance, by ignoring the past.

In response to criticism that the militants of 1968 did not have a program, Daniel Cohn-Bendit insists on the political effectiveness of being open before the future: "Everyone would be reassured, particularly Pompidou, if we set up a party and announced: 'All these people here are ours now. Here are our aims and this is how we are going to attain them.' They would know who they were dealing with and how to counter them. They could no longer have to face 'anarchy,' 'disorder,' 'uncontrollable effervescence.' " [31] Earlier in this interview with Sartre, Cohn-Bendit noted that "the Bolshevik Party did not 'lead' the Russian Revolution. It was borne along by the masses. It might have elaborated its theory *en route* and pushed the movement in one direction or another, but it did not by itself launch the movement." Cohn-Bendit could not speak so easily of "anarchy," "disorder," and "uncontrollable effervescence" if the ineluctable revolution that Marx had hypostatized was not imminent. "The revolution is thorough going [Marx tells us in *The Eighteenth Brumaire*]. It is still journeying through purgatory. It does its work methodically. By December 2, 1851 it had accomplished one half of its preparatory work; it is now accomplishing the other half. First it perfected the parliamentary power, in order to be able to overthrow it. Now that it has attained this it perfects the *executive power,* reduces it to its purest expression, isolates it, sets it up against itself as the sole target, in order to concentrate all its forces of destruction against it. And when it has done this second half of its preliminary work, Europe will leap from its seat and exultantly exclaim: 'Well grubbed, old mole.' " [32]

III

Until recently the antiutopian view has generally been associated with a conservative, even reactionary attitude. It is one of the ironies of the career of modern utopianism that what might be called the utopianism of reason has come to be seen as reactionary. Indeed, a new utopianism of the passional imagination has emerged with strong affinities with what I have characterized as antiutopianism. Such is the precariousness and fragility of ideas. Thus Herbert Marcuse can say much in the spirit of a Dostoevsky or a Zamiatin, though the idiom differs: "Self-consciousness and reason, which have conquered and shaped the historical world, have done so in the image of repression, internal and external. They have worked as the agents of domination." [33] Marcuse's immediate inspiration, of course, is Freud, or rather his version of Freud. Liberation can come only through the revolt of the repressed passions against the tyranny of reason. Though the philosophical bases vary, the new utopianism has its exponents in Marcuse, Norman O. Brown, R. D. Laing. One finds earlier versions in the surrealists, and one can go still further back to nineteenth century romanticism.* Even nineteenth century utopists like the Saint-Simonian Père Enfantin and of course Charles Fourier are in apparent revolt against

---

* The archetypal origins of the new utopianism are probably in the pursuit of the millennium that the heretical chiliastic sects of the Middle Ages were engaged in.

the rationalist bias of Enlightenment utopianism. Our recent counterculture has been in good part defined by the new utopianism. It is as if the antiutopian argument has been assimilated by those who refuse to abandon the utopian project of transforming the world, and so they attempt to imagine a counterutopia, which will express the human energies that the utopia of reason denies.

Antiutopianism differs from the new utopianism in two respects. First, while utopianism is committed to transforming life, its antagonist dramatizes the losses incurred by the transformation. Zamiatin wants to preserve or recover "the wild hurricane of ancient life," [34] the disturbing pulsations of green life beyond the glass wall that the rationalized technological society erects, the feeling of "warm red blood" coursing in the veins against all utopian effort to eliminate these elements of life or to convert them to beneficent purposes by exorcising what is painful and disorderly in them. Antiutopianism resists all effort to convert tragedy to reason—or happiness, harmony, order (which are cognate terms). Zamiatin's irony directed toward the sexual project of utopia (expressed through the as yet innocent consciousness of his hero) is characteristic. "The thing which was for the ancients a source of innumerable stupid tragedies has been converted in our time into a harmonious, agreeable and useful function like sleep, physical labor, the taking of food, digestion etc. etc. Hence you see how the great power of logic purifies everything it happens to touch. Oh, if only you unknown readers can conceive this divine power! If you will only learn to follow it to the end!" [35]

Second, antiutopianism resists the generalizing impulse of utopianism—which it sees as coercive because of its vision of the irreducible and unpredictable variety of human energy, need, aspiration. The hero's beloved in *We* compares man to a novel: "up to the last page one does not know what the end will be. It would not be worth reading otherwise." [36] Utopian fiction and parodically antiutopian fiction present a schematic environment and schematic characters. In *We* Zamiatin's hero is simply the man of feeling who resists the tyranny of reason. The variables are limited in order to assure predictability.

The utopian feeling for system is anathema to the antiutopian view. Utopist Charles Fourier, whose work does honor to the appetites and the passions, in particular the sexual passion, and who perceived the coerciveness of the philosophical habit of generalizing about human needs, appetites, and passions, nevertheless succumbs to rationalistic presumptions about totality and unity. The extraordinary variety of human passions (which Fourier described in detail) could not only be expressed and satisfied according to specified relationships and associations in phalansteries; these relationships and associations could in turn be reconciled to a conception of totality, unity, and harmony. The extravagance of Fourier's performance, which has made him something of a buffoon in the intellectual history of the nineteenth century, is precisely in the ease with which he could reconcile in his mind (the incurable vice of rationalism asserting itself once more) his remarkable perception of individual passions (for which he was admired by no less a connoisseur than Balzac) and his belief in totality and unity. In Fourier's dream of liberation, the passions conveniently divest themselves of their pain and their ferocity.

The question remains whether the antiutopian predilection for uniqueness and variety—its intolerance of the generalized coercive ideal—is entirely consistent. Zamiatin's formulation of revolutionary freedom contains a problem of which he is apparently unaware, a problem that will plague the counterutopianism of the passional imagination. Who wants, who needs the turbulence, the dangerous depths of the passional life? A substantial creative minority perhaps (intellectuals, artists, revolutionary heroes, saints), and perhaps its gifted, sympathetic following. Most people do not seem to want it. On Zamiatin's own account they prefer the sleeping sickness that the utopia of reason offers. When Zamiatin says they "must not be allowed to sleep," is he not in danger of performing the proctorial role that Marx and the vanguard of the proletariat performed for the proletariat, and thus in effect proposing a coercive higher reason that endangers the very principle of freedom—for instance, the freedom to sleep?

The Imagination and the Temptations of Politics

The modern belief that art can change life has its origins in the late eighteenth century. For the *homme de lettres* of the Enlightenment the imagination of a world in which man is freed from political tyranny and religious dogma is the work of reason. Since the nineteenth century, freedom has increasingly found its voice through the poetic imagination, the faculty to which the romantics gave priority, indeed to which they often opposed reason itself.

The authority of the imagination has its basis in the belief that it can transform the world or even realize it. This is a theme that runs through romantic theorizing about poetry, however different the various theories might be. Blake's view that the world is not real until it has been made over by the imagination, Coleridge's idea that the primary act of perception (let alone the secondary act of creation) is itself an act of imagination, Shelley's vision of the chaos of the modern world being redeemed by the values of the imagination (the poet in the *Defense of Poetry* is figured as a law-giver), all have in common a view of the imagination as a transforming action in the world.

One of the most impressive early formulations of the political project of the artistic imagination can be found in Friedrich Schiller's letters *On the Aesthetic Education of Man,* published in 1795 at the time of the Reign of Terror. The philosophical status of the work is dubious, though it has won the respect of philosophers, notably Hegel, who greatly admired it. (More recently, Herbert Marcuse has alluded to it as an anticipation of his own work.) It is not hard to see what the objections of analytically oriented philosophers would be to the text. The use of terms does not seem consistent, the distinctions do not always settle long enough to hold up to logical scrutiny, the argument is often elusively abstract. My interest in the text, of course, is not as a philosopher. I will consider the work in the aspects in which its influence has been most profound and most relevant to our situation: partly as cultural criticism and partly as manifesto. Indeed Schiller seems to be addressing himself to the contemporary situation: "Expectantly the gaze of philosopher and man of the world alike is fixed on the political scene, where now, so it is believed, the very fate of mankind is being debated. Does it not betray a culpable indifference to the commonweal not to take part in this general debate? . . . I hope to convince you that the theme I have chosen is far less alien to the needs of our age than to its taste. More than this: if man is ever to solve that problem of politics in practice he will have to approach it through the problem of the aesthetic, because it is only through Beauty that man makes his way to Freedom." [1] Schiller proposes a cultural revolution that can be read at once as an anticipation and a critique of current notions of cultural revolution.

In contrast to the view in which "utility is the great idol of the age . . . to which all talent must pay homage," Schiller proposes a view of art as autonomous, transcending the material claims of society. "Art must abandon actuality and soar with becoming boldness over wants and needs; for Art is a daughter of Freedom, and takes her orders from the necessity inherent in minds, not from the exigencies of matter." [2] The nonutilitarian view is not original, and in the nineteenth century it will become familiar, virtually a cliché of cultural criticism. What is compelling in Schiller's argument is the insistence on the political relevance of art in its condition of autonomy. Art is not useful to the political order, it is the vantage point from which the political life is judged and perhaps transformed.

Seen from the aesthetic point of view, the political realm

is the work of the "pedagogic and political artist," which Schiller distinguishes from "the fine artist" by the absolute respect he shows for the material of his art: "The consideration [the statesman-artist] must accord to its uniqueness and individuality is not merely subjective, and aimed at creating an illusion for the senses, but objective and directed to its innermost being." [3] It is the mark of the political despot that he treats man's idiosyncrasy and personality as if it were stone or wood or canvas to be shaped and imposed upon the arbitrary imagination of the despot. The political artist, in Schiller's view, must reject the despotism that violates personality, on the one hand, and the "savagery" and "barbarism" of the uncultivated self, on the other.* But the problem of savagery and barbarism has no direct political solution. It cannot be eliminated by political repression (the reactionary "solution") or by the political postulation of a new man (the solution of modern radicalism). "All improvement in the political sphere is to proceed from the ennobling of character—but how under the influence of a barbarous constitution is character ever to become ennobled? To this end we should, presumably, have to seek out some instrument not provided by the State, and to open up living springs which, whatever the political corruption, would remain clean and pure." [4] That instrument Schiller calls an aesthetic education.

An aesthetic education is at once a critical instrument and the *via media* toward moral fulfillment. Schiller exemplifies its critical character in dealing with the passion for justice. "The misfortunes of the human race speak urgently to the man of feeling; its degradation more urgently still . . . and

---

* Schiller distinguishes the savage, the barbarian, and the cultured man in the following manner: "The savage despises Civilization, and acknowledges Nature as his sovereign mistress. The barbarian derides and dishonours Nature, but, more contemptible than the savage, as often as not continues to be the slave of his slave. The man of Culture makes a friend of Nature, and honours her freedom while curbing only her caprice" (*On the Aesthetic Education of Man,* ed. and trans. Wilkinson and Willoughby, p. 2).

in vigorous souls ardent love drives impatiently on towards action. But did he ever ask himself whether those disorders in the moral world offend his reason, or whether they do not rather wound his self-love?" [5] An aesthetic education criticizes the basis for the passion for justice, attempts to distinguish between what Nietzsche was later to call resentment from the disinterested desire to right wrongs. The aesthetic project of ennobling character would foster disinterestedness. It is of course a pragmatic question whether the passion for justice can be sustained for long without resentment. Schiller's view is that it is precisely the task of an aesthetic education to exorcise resentment or self-congratulation from the passion for justice, so that it remains free from cruelty. If this exorcism cannot be achieved, the aesthetic critique might have the effect of freezing the passion for justice. Knowing this, one at any given moment might still be willing to pay the price of resentment for action. But whether one chooses to listen or to ignore the aesthetic critique at any given moment, it unquestionably provides a permanent insight into the kind of action that leads to revolution and radical change.

The political effect of Schiller's insistence that political liberation must await the aesthetic transformation of man is in a sense conservative or at least antirevolutionary. Schiller is strenuously opposed to the disruptions, the discontinuities to which the political revolutionary imagination is committed. What he is proposing is a cultural revolution that has paradoxically a conservative respect for the complex living character of society. "What we must chiefly bear in mind, then, is that physical society in time must never for a moment cease to exist while moral society as idea is in the process of being formed; that for the sake of a man's moral dignity his actual existence must never be jeopardized. When the craftsman has a timepiece to repair, he can let its wheels run down; but the living clockwork of the state must be repaired while it is still striking, and it is a question of changing the revolving wheel while it revolves. For this reason a support must be looked for which will ensure the continuance of society, and make it independent of the Nature State which is to be abolished." [6]

Schiller's project is at once utopian and evolutionary. His "evolutionism" implicitly favors the existing "social constitution," however barbarous he believes it to be, over any revolutionary creation of a new constitution. He is prepared to endure the barbarities of the existing social condition (the natural condition) while awaiting attendance on the aesthetic education of man, rather than endorse the universal demand for political rights before man is morally prepared for them. He would seem to believe that the social constitution and its agents are as morally unprepared as those outside the political life who are clamoring for entry into it. And yet he does not want to risk the insurgence of what he calls from aristocratic prejudice "the lower and more numerous classes (in which crude, lawless impulses [have been] unleashed)." [7] The value of existing society (however barbarous its manifestations) is that it provides a social alternative to the chaos of an aesthetically unprepared revolution.

The aesthetic education is at once an instrument to resist the corruptions of man's actual political condition and the fulfillment or the vehicle of fulfillment of his dream of happiness. The happiness of this condition Schiller expresses through the phrase "the play impulse" or the instinct for play. Like Huizinga, Marcuse, and Brown after him, Schiller rescues the idea of play from frivolity. The seriousness of man's playfulness in the aesthetic state is that he achieves spontaneity and freedom of his full nature: its sensuous or material side and its intellectual or formal side. "He had learned to desire more nobly, so that he may not need to will sublimely." * The characteristic stress in the letters is on the integration of man's powers, in which each power is

---

* Schiller's distinction between the (authentically) moral and the aesthetic does not hold up in my reading of the letters. "Man in his physical state merely suffers the dominion of nature; he emancipates himself from this dominion in the aesthetic state, and he acquires mastery over it in the moral" (*On the Aesthetic Education of Man*, p. 171). The moral and the aesthetic become indistinguishable in Schiller.

strengthened without the other power suffering any diminishment. "For if the sensuous drive becomes the determining one, that is to say, if the senses assume the role of legislator and the world suppresses the Person, then the world ceases to be an object precisely to the extent that it becomes a force." "The formal drive must not be the result of spiritual impotence or flabbiness of thought or will; for this would only degrade man. It must, if it is to be at all praiseworthy, spring from abundance of feeling and sensation. Sense herself must, with triumphant power, remain mistress of her own domain, and resist the violence which the mind, by its usurping tactics, would fain inflict upon her. In a single word: Personality must keep the sensuous drive within its proper bounds, and receptivity, or Nature, must do the same with the formal drive." The political consequence of this fulfilled integration of all human powers is a noble freedom. "The things he possesses, the things he produces, may no longer bear upon them the marks of their use . . . Disinterested and undirected pleasure is now numbered among the necessities of existence, and what is in fact unnecessary soon becomes the best part of his delight." And again: "In the Aesthetic State everything—even the tool which serves—is a free citizen, having equal rights with the noblest; and the mind, which would force the patient mass beneath the yoke of its purposes, must here first obtain its assent. Here, therefore, in the realm of Aesthetic Semblance we find that ideal of equality fulfilled which the Enthusiast would fain see realized in substance." The aesthetic hero is without envy or servility or savagery, because he is self-delighted.[8]

What is interesting in Schiller's performance, from a political point of view, is the way he affirms aristocratic value in the service of a democratic enterprise. Unlike Nietzsche, Schiller stresses the graciousness rather than the ferocity of the strong toward the weak. "Now weakness becomes sacred, and unbridled strength dishonourable; the injustice of nature is rectified by the magnanimity of the chivalric code."[9] Schiller, however, is not guilty of that Christian and modern sentimentality that pretends that weakness is strength or that refuses to make distinctions among various orders of strength and weakness. He does not confuse his desire for the widest possible diffusion of an aesthetic education with his judgment of who does or does not have a share in "the state of beauty." The conclusion of the aesthetic letters is appropriately paradoxical: "But does such a State of Aesthetic Semblance really exist: And if so, where is it to be found? As a need, it exists in every finely attuned soul; as a realized fact, we are likely to find it, like the pure Church and the pure Republic, only in some few chosen circles . . . where men make their way, with undismayed simplicity and tranquil innocence, through even the most involved and complex situations, free alike of the compulsion to infringe the freedom of others in order to assert their own, as of the necessity to shed their dignity in order to manifest Grace." [10] Or reversing the perspective, it is democracy aspiring to the aristocratic condition of grace and freedom, without any assurance that this condition can be achieved by "the lower and more numerous classes."

If that assurance cannot be given, it becomes a real question whether "the path of aesthetics" is the way of political freedom. For even if a happy few are to achieve that noble integration of all their powers that Schiller sees as the condition of true freedom, what political meaning can this freedom have in a society whose constitution remains barbarous and whose people remain political barbarians and savages?

In the enthusiasm of the discovery of the creative powers of the imagination (which he shared with his generation) Schiller expresses what is to become a characteristic ambition of art and culture to redeem the world of politics. Less grandiosely, and in quite different terms, Matthew Arnold shared that ambition for English society, when in *A French Eton* he envisaged a redeemed society in terms of a "cultured, ennobled, transformed middle class" and a working class provided with "a practicable passage to . . . the joy and beauty of life." [11] Despite Schiller's utopian ambitions for art and culture, he had a clear perception of the possible insusceptibility of the masses to the redemptive action of art. He did not suffer as we do now from the populist piety about the creativity of everyman either as a maker of art or as an object of its grace—if only, as the countercultural argument goes, the political and economic opportunities for creativity existed for everyone. Nor does he suffer from the current confusion between actuality and possibility. The "state of beauty" he envisaged for man could not simply be taken for granted. Controlled by a "conservative" feeling for the cultural process, he could not sanction the assuming of rights, the creation of a new polis for which men were not ready. Though his argument seems to be an early version of the psychology of liberation fostered by Marcuse and Brown and though it has democratic ambitions, it is distinguished by its refusal to identify in a revolutionary way the need for liberation with the assertion that liberation is at hand. Liberation has to be nurtured like a plant, to use an organic simile that would have suited Schiller.

What is permanently problematic in Schiller's argument is its essential implicit claim—that one can exfoliate an authentic ideal of a noble, just and free political community from the aesthetic imagination. There is a deliberate abstractness in Schiller's thought that precludes either a demonstration or refutation of its possibility. Schiller himself concedes that in the history of cultures there is strong evidence that during periods of high artistic activity the integrity of political life seems to suffer. Imagining a condition in which "sense [sensuousness] . . . remain [s] mistress of her own domain, and resist [s] the violence which the mind, by its usurping tactics, would fain inflict upon her," he is at the same time conceiving a mind (as yet unrealized) sufficiently powerful and resilient to be enhanced by "the fulness of sensations." Mind or what Schiller calls the formal impulsion is tempered, not overthrown, by sensations. Though Schiller scrupulously makes a distinction between the empirical and the ideal (he condemns as pernicious what he calls

132

"the premature striving for harmony" between mind and nature) the effect of this kind of speculation has been to create enormous credit in our cultural life for the political claim of the imagination.

What makes the claim dubious is not simply the apparently corruptive effects of art on political life (which Schiller, following Rousseau, acknowledges as a mark of our barbarous civilization) but the unmistakable symptoms of political barbarism in the character of the artist, of the imagination, and of the work of art itself, where one would hope to find anticipations of the ideal polity. Even those who have created works of art—works that presumably would contribute to "the state of beauty" that Schiller conceives as necessary for the good political life—have often lacked nobility not only in their lives but in their imaginations as well. One has only to consider a political order constituted by the imagination of a D. H. Lawrence or a Marinetti or a Yeats or an Artaud—all imaginations of imperfect virtue to put it generously—to see how difficult at the very least is the hope that art or culture will redeem the polis.

The poet is usually content to confine his political fantasies in a work of art. Or the fantasies might find their way into a personal statement. Surrealism has been an exceptional attempt to turn the cause of the imagination into a political movement—and is therefore an instructive instance for any consideration of the political ambitions of an aesthetic education. "The poet of the future," wrote André Breton, the founder and guiding spirit of surrealism, "will go beyond the depressing idea of the irreparable divorce between action and dream. He will bring together, at whatever cost, the two terms of the relationship which, if destroyed, would instantly cause the most precious conquests to become a dead letter." [12] The romantics were content to express the dream life; for Breton poetry is the agent for realizing it. Not only does the surrealist want to break out of the prison of language and reason into action and the experience of what is unknown and marvellous, but he sees himself en-

gaged in a movement, a collective enterprise that will transform social as well as personal life. (Breton once characterized the surrealist movement as "an association such as has
not been seen, as far as its goals and enthusiasms were concerned, at least since Saint-Simonism." [13])

In utopian fashion, the surrealists conceive reality
futuristically—not as a given, but as a fulfillment of the
imagination. Commonplace reality is denied, overcome by
the power of poetry. Paul Eluard writes:

> From the chrysalises of my eyes
> Will be born my shadowy double
> Speaking with his back to the light
>   suspecting divinity
> He overwhelms the real
> And I subdue the world in a black
>   mirror
> And I imagine my power.[14]

And Breton makes the case for the imagination in utopian
terms: "To reduce imagination to slavery—even if one's so-
called happiness is at stake—means to violate all that one
finds in one's inmost self of ultimate justice. Imagination
alone tells me what can be." [15] On first blush the word "justice" surprises, because of its rational and repressive associations. But it is Breton's implicit point that the rational conception of justice is inadequate because repressive. Real
justice consists in giving free rein to impulses and passions
(in practicing poetry)—that is, in the freedom to be and to
act out all that one is.

The political expression of surrealism would appear to be
anarchism. "The mere word 'freedom' is the only one that
excites me," Breton asserts. "The imagination is perhaps on
the point of reasserting itself, or reclaiming its rights." And
Breton links the exercise of the imagination not with order
or harmony but with anarchy. "Man proposes and disposes.
He and he alone can determine whether he is completely
master of himself, that is, whether he maintains the body of
his desires, daily more formidable, in a state of anarchy." [16]

For Breton anarchy is not simply a political metaphor for the operations for the imagination, it is the life force that must manifest itself everywhere in the political sphere as well as the artistic sphere. Breton is pleased to report that the International Surrealist Exhibition in June 1936 opened at the very moment that "French workers were employing for the first time tactics quite unpremediated on their part . . . forcibly occupying factories." [17] He speaks of the "spontaneity and suddenness of this departure" and sees in the ability of the action to "spread widely and swiftly" the promise "that nothing can prevent it from attaining its immediate aims."

For all their loquacity, the statements in the manifestoes of surrealism are curiously unsatisfying, for they indicate very little of the moral energy of the anarchic imagination. We are deliberately shocked to be told that the classic surrealist gesture is the random firing of a pistol into a crowd (the shock is in Breton's insistence that the assertion is not a symbolic one), but he is irritatingly elusive in accounting— or rather not accounting—for what this means for the political ambitions of surrealism. He chooses rather to play the old aesthetic game of *épater le bourgeois* by deliberately baffling the philistine's expectation of lucid good sense. Schiller would doubtless have recoiled from such an exemplification of the passional imagination. To be sure, Schiller did not have access to Freud's explorations. He could not have been as impressed with the sheer violence of unconscious life as were Breton and his surrealist comrades. Nor did he share the surrealist loathing of the Cartesian *cogito*, which he doubtless would have invoked to contain the violence. In the surrealist view, an honest commitment to the imagination is a courageous commitment to its violence. But how does the firing of a pistol into the crowd redeem the social world?

Breton perhaps felt that the surrealists could play out their violent fantasies, because the actual task of making the revolution belonged to the Bolsheviks. (Breton and his surrealist friends—though not all of them—offer us the remarkable anomaly of a Bolshevik anarchism.) But this does not satisfy on surrealist terms, because it makes the surrealist imagination, indeed the imagination itself, politically irrelevant. The fact is that the imagination to which the surrealists were honestly committed is profoundly antipathetic to the political ideals they upheld as Bolsheviks: the liberation of the proletariat and the creation of a new communal life.

What characterizes surrealist imagination is not simply its violence, but its indomitable egotism as well. To see this we have to go to utterances that reveal the surrealist fantasy. In *Paysan de Paris* Louis Aragon defines "the vice called surrealism" as "the disordered and impassioned use of the image as a drug, or rather the uncontrolled provocation of the image for itself and for what it brings with it, in the domain of representation, by way of unforseeable perturbation and metamorphosis: for each image each time forces you to revise the Universe. And there is for each man an image that needs to be found to annihilate the whole Universe." [18] And when the world is annihilated Aragon discovers that "there is no longer room here except for me."

The act of imagination is the unfolding of desire, which has giant roots in our unconscious, roots we glimpse only in our dreams. The substance of poetry is the dream life. Aragon once more: [19]

> Le vent qui reve sur la mer
> Je dit RÊVE
> Rè-é-eve.
>
> The wind that dreams on the sea
> I say DREAM
> Dre-e-e-am.

The word expands as the self expands:

> Je m'étends je m'étends par des chemins etranges
> Mon ombre se denatte et tout se denature
> Le forêt de mes mains s'enflamme
> Mes cheveux chantent.

I extend myself, I extend myself along strange roads
My shadow unravels itself and everything denatures itself
The forest of my hands catches fire
My hair sings.

Nothing here suggests interest in or possible reconciliation with a communal ethic. If each man aspires to become his own universe, the space for social life will disappear indeed.

The sheer aggressiveness of the dream life, which is for the surrealists the sacred source of poetic energy and which they want realized, is celebrated in "Ton Portrait," a poem by Aimé Cesaire, written during his surrealist period. The poem invokes the river of dream which is seen as "a patient royal crocodile," a "royal anaconda" and more terribly "as the source of nightmare the most Pelean mountains," Pelée being a volcanic mountain in Martinique that erupted in 1902 and killed everybody in adjacent areas except one prisoner in an underground jail. Cesaire calls to the "river / to whom all is permitted" asking it "above all carry away my banks / widen me." [20]

How do we explain the incongruity between the commitment to a collectivist politics and the extreme libidinous egotism of the surrealists? I have referred to the curious anomaly of surrealism's link with Bolshevism, primarily though not exclusively in its Trotskyite version. There are a number of adventitious reasons for this. The fact that the first socialist revolution was led by the Bolsheviks gave them their preeminent authority as revolutionaries. Moreover, despite the disillusioning experience of Stalinist terror and cultural philistinism, the intellectual personality of Trotsky offered an alternative within the Bolshevik dispensation. Surrealists like Paul Eluard and René Char returned to the fold of the Communist Party after World War II because of the exemplary role the party played in the Resistance. But these are adventitious reasons, for they do not explain why the surrealists would be attracted to the Bolshevik cause on the basis of their own imaginative experience.

In fact, in cultural matters Bolshevism posed an immense problem for surrealism. Having always insisted on the revolutionary practice of poetry, on the need for acting out the word, and having found in Bolshevism the revolutionary ideology par excellence, surrealism, it would seem, would find its fulfillment in Bolshevism. And yet Breton's artistic and spiritual instincts made him resist the Bolshevik appropriation of surrealism, for the cultivation of the inner life, the attempt to discover, enrich, and act it out (the perennial work of culture), had little place in Bolshevik ideology—indeed, was suspect as a form of bourgeois subjectivism. Breton maintained his paradoxical position by insisting on surrealism and Bolshevism as parallel movements, complementing one another. "All of us seek to shift power from the hands of the bourgeoisie to those of the proletariat. Meanwhile, it is nonetheless necessary that the experiments of inner life continue, and do so, of course, without external or even Marxist control." [21] The theoretical and practical consequences of this position are not worked out: what if the movements are not parallel, what if the acted out experiences of inner life seriously impinge on the requirements of the Bolshevik revolution, both before and after its triumph. Indeed, could any two aesthetic programs be less reconcilable than surrealism and socialist realism?

Yet the surrealist attraction to Bolshevism, I suspect, was not merely a matter of finding itself on the common ground of opposition to capitalism. It expresses, I think, an impulse in the surrealists that contradicts its essential anarchic individualistic tendency. A clue to this might be found in the artistic politics of Breton. The role of Breton in the movement was not unlike the role of the party chief, enforcing discipline, scolding members for deviations, expelling them from the movement when they proved to be incorrigible. This is a remarkable phenomenon when one considers statements like this: "Surrealism, such as I conceive it, asserts our complete nonconformism." [22] Apparently surrealism is nonconformist vis-à-vis the rest of the world, but surrealists must conform to an internal moral and aesthetic discipline—as defined by the party chief. Given Breton's antiphilistine esprit and the absence of police terror to back up his dicta, the personal authority of Breton, contradictory as it may seem to the logic of surrealism, gave surrealism its seriousness, its profound sense of responsibility and humanity.

Could it be that the very extremity of the libidinous surrealist desire for freedom—the intense need to venture into the domain of unconscious life and risk its terrors as well as its marvels, the passion to satisfy all desires—had to be counteracted by an almost chaste superegoistic insistence on the constructive, humane, and even social uses of surrealist activity? The favorite adversaries of surrealism were the cultural philistinisms of the bourgeoisie and the Stalinists, but Breton had a formidable enemy within, or rather a half friend, half enemy: the dadaism out of which surrealism itself emerged. Breton had broken with Tristan Tzara, the chief of dada, because dadaism represented for him a sterile and nihilistic gesture. The classic surrealist gesture, the random firing of a pistol into a crowd, is, I think, a vestige of the dadaistic legacy in surrealism, which Breton sought to preserve because it conveys so vividly the intransigent commitment to the expression of energy at all costs. Consequently Breton's apparently perverse insistence on the literalness of his belief in the gesture. But the side of Breton that committed him to an active belief in a new political and social order could hardly allow this gesture to remain unchecked.

Surrealism as a self-conscious movement is dead. The literary remains consist of the manifestoes, experiments in introspection, not very many good poems. The doctrine of poetry as an action is, it seems to me, sufficiently fudged in the discussions to elude some of the challenge I have offered to surrealism. Certainly in contrast with the Bolshevik program the revolutionary actions of surrealism seem "merely" concerned with the inner lives of poet and reader. And yet if this is the case, the powerful urge in surrealism to exteriorize the inner life (Vincent Bounoure, a little known surrealist poet, defines reality as the satisfaction of desire[23]) does not seem accounted for. (The French students in 1968 took the surrealists seriously in their slogan "take your dreams for reality.")

If the movement is dead, the profound cultural impulse it incarnated is still very much alive. Indeed, the obscuring of implications in surrealism is a continuing fact of our cultural and political life. The problem still remains: what happens to the passional imagination when it precipitates itself into the practical political sphere? Is its action beneficent, humane, redemptive? The answers of Herbert Marcuse, Norman O. Brown, R. D. Laing, and the counterculture over which they preside are the same as the answer of the surrealists: a resounding affirmation. "Orpheus and Narcissus," Marcuse ruefully remarks, "have not become the culture-heroes of the Western world; the voice which does not command but sings; the gesture which offers and receives; the deed which is peace and ends the labor of conquest; the liberation from time which unites man with god, man and nature." [24] For Norman O. Brown the imagination is the exclusive instrument of revolutionary change. "In the dialectical view . . . demystification becomes the discovery of a new mystery . . . The next generation needs to be told that the real fight is not the political fight, but to put an end to politics. From politics to poetry . . . Poetry, art, imagination, the creator spirit is life itself; the revolutionary power to change the world." [25] And Theodore Roszak, summing it up for the counter culture, asserts: "Brown and Marcuse, you and I, most of us, perhaps all of us who must now begin to dig our way out from under the ancient and entrenched estrangement of our being; how dare *we* specify the limits of the real while we stand on the benighted side of liberation?" [26]

Lionel Trilling has shrewdly remarked apropos of R. D. Laing, whose equivocal sanctioning of a kind of insanity—holy poetic madness—puts him in the company of Marcuse and Brown, that many of those who respond to his doctrine, who desperately need the doctrine, "don't have it in mind to go mad, let alone insane." [27] But the reason for saying no to the question of whether the imagination redeems politics is not simply that the idea is impossible or fatuous. It is that in considering its political implications, its possibility, we become aware of its perniciousness. Stated in aesthetic terms, the perniciousness of the doctrine is in the rejection of the metaphoric character of poetry for "the image as drug" (to use Aragon's phrase) and as action: it is in the deliberate confounding of the life of the imagination with the practical life.

The boldness of the imagination (which Breton and the surrealists affirm) is possible only if one can distinguish between the imagination and practical life, because the imperial egotism of the imagination tends to be coercive and tyrannical in a political context real or imagined, inadvertent as this tyranny might be. The imagination is an anarchist, as Breton rightly claims. But it is an anarchist (he did not note) of the aristocratic variety: powerfully vital, expansive, concerned to fulfill itself even at the expense of the other. (The intransigent hatred of the bourgeois in Breton owes as much to the "aristocratic" bias of the nineteenth century artist who believed himself to be the repository of spiritual values as it does to his sympathy with the oppressed working class.) Vitality, we know, can have a coercive effect on the less vital, indeed, often thrives at the expense of the less vital. So long as this vitality is contained by the imagination or by the individual personality, it constitutes the incarnation of a valuable life possibility. The problem arises when what I would call the aristocratic anarchism of the imagination ceases to be an individual phenomenon, when the strong personality ceases simply to assert himself for his own sake and tries to give to his will the force of the collectivity. What is essentially an acting out of an individual destiny becomes confused with the problem of creating or sustaining a political community. Since the imagination rarely troubles to articulate the structure of the polity, what we usually have are expressions of energies and attitudes that become the aesthetic basis for despotism. D. H. Lawrence, who did take the trouble to suggest the structure of a society, comes out as a kind of platonist in whose scheme life values (rather than merely rational values) are preserved by an elite of the gifted and the imaginative, while the rest of society performs the necessary social and economic functions. In a curious appropriation of Ivan Karamazov's dream of the Grand Inquisitor, Lawrence turns the Grand Inquisitor's argument into a justification of mistrust for what Nietzsche calls "the herd" and of the necessity of protecting the freedom and power of the few from the presumption that all men are capable of perfection. "So let the specially gifted few make the decision between good and and evil and establish the life values against the money values. And let the many accept the decision, with gratitude, and bow down to the few, in the hierarchy." [28]

Perhaps the most striking revelation of the tyrannical side of the imagination in modern times is Marinetti's notorious Manifesto of Futurism.

1. We want to sing the love of danger, the habit of energy and rashness.
2. The essential elements of our poetry will be courage, audacity and revolt.
3. Literature has up to now magnified pensiveness, immobility, ecstasy and slumber. We want to exalt the movements of aggression, feverish sleeplessness, the double march, the perilous leap, the slap and the blow with the fist.
4. We declare that the splendour of the world has been enriched by new beauty: the beauty of speed. A racing automobile with its bonnet adorned with great tubes like serpents with explosive breath . . . a roaring motor which seems to run on machine-gun fire is more beautiful than the Victory of Samothrace.
5. We want to sing the man at the wheel, the ideal axis of which crosses the earth, itself hurled along its orbit.
6. The poet must spend himself with warmth, glamour and prodigality to increase the enthusiastic fervour of the primordial elements.
7. Beauty exists only in struggle. There is no masterpiece that

has not an aggressive character. Poetry must be a violent assault on the forces of the unknown, to force them to bow down before man.

8. We are the extreme promontory of the centuries! What is the use of looking behind at the moment when we must open the mysterious shutters of the impossible? Time and space died yesterday. We are already living in the absolute, since we have already created eternal, omnipresent speed.

9. We want to glorify war—the only cure for the world—militarism, patriotism, the destructive gesture of the anarchists, the beautiful ideas which kill, and contempt for woman.

10. We want to demolish museums and libraries, fight morality, feminism and all opportunist and utilitarian cowardice.

11. We will sing of great crowds agitated by work, pleasure and revolt; the multi-coloured and polyphonic surf of revolutions in modern capitals: the nocturnal vibration of the arsenals and the workshops beneath their violent electric moons: the gluttonous railway stations devouring smoking serpents; the factories suspended from the clouds by the thread of their smoke; bridges with the leap of gymnasts flung across the diabolic cutlery of sunny rivers: the adventurous steamers sniffing the horizon; greatbreasted locomotives, puffing on the rails like enormous steel horses with long tubes for bridle, and the gliding flight of aeroplanes whose propellor sounds like the flapping of a flag and the applause of enthusiastic crowds.[29]

Marinetti goes on to characterize the manifesto as one "of ruinous and incendiary violence." He looks forward to young men who will carry the futurist banner. "And strong healthy Injustice will shine radiantly from their eyes. For art can only be violence, cruelty and injustice."

This, of course, is the aesthetic of fascism. "The destructive gesture of the anarchist" is not directed against an immoral and unjust society (an argument anarchists of socialist and democratic persuasion would use to justify terroristic activity), it expresses rather the power of steel, it glorifies war. The virtues celebrated are the aristocratic virtues: "love of danger, the habit of energy and rashness, courage and audacity." Though fascism may be hostile to these virtues when the "destructive anarchist" chooses to direct his activity against the fascist state, it is not difficult to see how these "virtues" can be used to support the state. What they amount to when the anarchist is in possession of the state is the power to crush enemies within and without.

If the Futurist attitude does not take a fascist form in the Soviet poet Vladimir Mayakovsky (whose violent behavior outraged even Marinetti), it is because it is counteracted by a lacerating masochism in which the aggression is turned inward and because the aggressive energy could find a sublimation in the Bolshevik revolution. But Mayakovsky does give us the pure Futurist attitude from time to time. First, the unbounded egotism: *

> I feel
> my "I"
> is much too small for me.
> Stubbornly a body pushes out of me.
>
> Glorify me!
> For me the great are no match.
> Upon every achievement
> I stamp *nihil.*
>
> I never want to read anything.
> Books?
> What are books!
>
> I spit on the fact
> that neither Homer nor Ovid
> invented characters like us,
> pock-marked with soot.
> I know
> the sun would dim, on seeing
> the gold fields of our souls!

And the violence:

> How dare you call yourself a poet,
> and twitter grayly like a quail!

* Mayakovsky's work (his poems as well as aesthetic) is, to be sure, not simply an expression of strident egotism. In *How Verses Are Made,* for example, Mayakovsky comes across as an almost modest, hardworking Bolshevik practitioner of the art—a manufacturer of verse, in Mayakovsky's own idiom. But the strident egotism is a strong and essential element of his poetry.

> This day
> brass knuckles
> must
> split the world inside the skull! [30]

The immoralism of Futurism, to be sure, does not exhaust the possibilities of the cult of imagination. But the attitude it exhibits has been a strong element in the modern imagination, which no theory of political and cultural renewal based on the passional imagination can afford to ignore. It is not fortuitous, for example, that so many imaginative artists found themselves attracted to fascism in its early stages. As I argued earlier, modern criticism has not been very illuminating on this subject. Its insistence on separating political and aesthetic matters has often made it overlook the political implications of the act of imagination. To see the politics in or of a work as merely adventitious to its aesthetic authority is to ignore the strong possibility that the political implication of a work is bound up with the imaginative disposition of the artist. Modern criticism has not fully addressed itself to the question whether a Lawrence or a Yeats or a Pound could have had any other kind of politics given what they were as artists. The question is a difficult one. The veneration for tradition and for a fixed hierarchical society in writers like Eliot, Pound, and Wyndham Lewis are not a manifestation of the cult of imagination. In his Christian humility, Eliot could not possibly belong to the cult. Writers came to fascism from motives other than strictly aesthetic ones. There is, however, a strong presumption for the view that the aristocratic anarchism of the cult of imagination is an important motive, though not the only one, for the attraction to fascism.

I am not suggesting that fascism is the practical outcome of the cult of imagination. I am saying that the cult of imagination has become in one of its major manifestations an aesthetic justification for fascism. Nor am I suggesting that the imagination always and intrinsically has the ambition to destroy or make over the universe. The imagination has been

145

known to be content with itself, to delight in artistic objects of its own making. But there is the imagination that experiences itself as denied in the act of making the work of art—and discovers in the larger world an occasion for the satisfaction of its aggressive and erotic energies. This kind of imagination is tempted by the world of politics.

The attraction to fascism suggests the limits of the moral and spiritual authority of the imagination. Within the imaginative structure of the work noxious political implications can be suppressed, and it is only the philistine reader who would insist on holding the artist responsible for every practical consequence of the imagination. Throughout his career Yeats sought to create an imaginative space in which the self could achieve grace and freedom. To be sure, when this quest for freedom, imagined with such superb energy and invention, impinges upon the claims for freedom and justice made by the historically exploited or the less gifted the effect may be the reactionary politics we normally identify with Yeats. Yet we would not want to deny the value of that aspiration. Or if we did deny the aspiration, then we would perform that radical countercultural act that very few liberals, and not many radicals for that matter, are willing to perform, for despite their rejection or loathing of the politics they go on admiring, even loving, the superb aristocratic and imperial bearing of Yeats's poetry—admiring a quality missing, perhaps necessarily missing, from their daily lives.

Indeed, in reading Yeats's poetry or Nietzsche's aphorisms one finds oneself in continuous sympathy with what is being said (often to one's own surprise) because the reactionary statement is not animated by philistine smugness, narrow-minded materialism, misanthropic self-interest, or a cruel indifference to the sufferings of others.* More often than not, these are the targets of attack by the reactionary artist, and the attack is made in behalf of a great-souled sentiment of

---

* There is an aristocratic cruelty in writers like Nietzsche and Yeats that derives from a heroic perception of the murderous innocence of life.

human nobility. Even Pound's fascism was motivated by a vision of the profound corruption of European life, to which a radical of democratic persuasion might be able to give qualified assent. The recoil from fascism in writers initially attracted to it is a recoil from its deep rootedness in the philistine system it was supposed to have overthrown.

In asserting the need of the imagination to secure itself from the temptations of politics, I am not advocating the New Critical view that politics in literature is soluble subject matter that dissolves and loses its identity in an aesthetic solution. Quite to the contrary. The political subject matter—or the political effect of the work itself—may be sufficiently explosive to require that one resist any easy transference of the imagination to practical life. Transference of course necessarily occurs; indeed, it is a function of the power of the image or the drama or the character that the work may affect even the political will of the public. But it is a kind of guarantee of the freedom of the imagination that it can exercise itself in the implicit knowledge that it is not the equivalent of firing a pistol into the crowd. Immoralist art and thought, as Nietzsche so well understood, is experimental, not to be imitated by everyone and not to be given an immediate political realization. "He, however, who would dissect must kill, but only in order that we may know more, judge better, live better, not in order that all the world may dissect. Unfortunately men still think that every moralist in his action must be a pattern for others to imitate." [31] And Yeats, who never fully secured himself from the temptations of politics (Conor Cruse O'Brien and others have documented Yeats's courtship with fascism) nevertheless had a profound understanding of the need for keeping the imagination and politics separate. "The swan" which Yeats earlier in the poem "Nineteen Hundred and Nineteen" had compared to a solitary soul "has leaped into the desolate heaven."

> That image can bring wildness, bring a rage
> To end all things, to end
> What my laborious life imagined, even

> The half-imagined, the half-written page;
> O but we dreamed to mend
> Whatever mischief seemed
> To afflict mankind, but now
> That winds of winter blow
> Learn that we were crack-pated when we dreamed.[32]

The utopists of the passional imagination have simply postulated the beneficence of a recreation of political and social life on the basis of what Norman O. Brown calls the revolutionary poetic imagination. As I have tried to show, the reconstructed Dionysian ego (to use another phrase of Brown's) does not seem to offer much political wisdom for a whole society. Since these utopists are democrats, it is an important objection to their vision of society that the imagination may have a strong aristocratic bias. The objection can be put in a somewhat different form. Let us assume that the regime of the poetic imagination would not involve the direct coercion of the ungifted by the gifted. Since there is sufficient creative potentiality in everyone, a society in which the realization of it is made easier would not divide so easily between the gifted and the ungifted. The question still remains: who can become all that the poet dreams? Recall Rilke's ambition for politicizing, so to speak, the poetic imagination. "Not for all time will the artist live side by side with ordinary men. As soon as the artist—the more flexible and deeper type among them—becomes rich and virile, as soon as he *lives* what now he merely *dreams,* man will degenerate and gradually die out. The artist is eternity protruding into time." [33] The coercive element is, I think, in the ideal itself. For all its sensitivity to the organic and passional qualities of human life, its acute awareness of the disastrous ambitions of rationalistic utopias, contemporary romantic utopia may be especially for the young a Mephistophelean temptation, catering to our incurable desire to be Faust. The dream of "integral satisfaction" (Marcuse's phrase) may be after all the ambition of extraordinarily sensitive and passionate spirits whose fulfillment would be self-oppression for others. In an artist, hero, or saint the desire may be fruitful. As a democratic promise, it may turn out to be at best irrelevant and at worst a disastrous spur to those of little gift but of unlimited intellectual, imaginative, and moral ambition.

The opportunities created by a society for the cultivation of authentic individuality and creative power, the highest expression of that individuality, are as John Stuart Mill argued in his essay *On Liberty* a principal measure of the integrity and value of the society. Individuality is at once an end in itself and an essential condition for criticizing and enriching the quality of social life. The creative imaginations of poets and artists inevitably have a transforming effect on a society or a portion of society that permits susceptibility to artistic vision and utterance—though, of course, that effect cannot be specified in advance. Given the moral ambiguities of the poetic imagination, the argument for resisting some of its ambitions can be understood as an argument made in the interest of imagination as well as society—a statement that fits as well my cautionary argument against utopian logic. My criticism, like nemesis, is directed toward the hubris of reason and imagination, not toward reason and imagination themselves.

Ideology and Disinterestedness

Julien Benda's argument for the virtues of intellectual disinterestedness (in *The Treason of the Clerks,* 1927) is perhaps the last significant expression of the naïve nineteenth century faith in Absolute Truth and the possibility of an Olympian attachment to it. If Absolute Truth no longer exists, if objectivism is a myth even in scientific knowledge (as Michael Polanyi and Thomas Kuhn have persuasively argued), does intellectual disinterestedness have any meaning? Can we avoid the conclusion that we are left either with a skeptical relativism, which tends to deny authority to all intellectual and imaginative claims to truth, or to ideology, which is based on moral and political commitment?

Michael Polanyi, who through the years has made a powerful argument for the subjective element in knowledge, has at the same time argued for the need for continuing to foster self-perpetuating cultural elites. For Polanyi the conclusion is neither radical skepticism nor ideological partisanship, though his view of how independence of thought is sustained implies an ideological commitment of a kind. Polanyi writes:

Can we face the fact that, no matter how liberal a free society may be, it is also profoundly conservative? This is a fact.
The recognition granted in a free society to the independent growth of science, art and morality, involves a dedication of society to the fostering of a specific tradition of thought, transmitted and cultivated by a particular group of authoritative specialists, perpetuating themselves by co-option. To uphold the independence of thought implemented by such a society is to subscribe to a kind of orthodoxy which, though it specifies no

fixed articles of faith, is virtually unassailable within the limits imposed on the process of innovation by the cultural leadership of a free society . . .

Must this institutional framework be accepted as the civic home of a free society? Is it true that the absolute right of moral self-determination, on which political liberty was founded, can be upheld only by refraining from any radical actions towards the establishment of justice and brotherhood? That indeed, unless we agree that within our lifetime we must no more loosen the ties of a free society, however iniquitous they may be, we shall inevitably precipitate men into an abject servitude.

For my part, I would say: Yes. I believe that, on the whole, these limitations are imperative. Unjust privileges prevailing in a free society can be reduced only by carefully graded stages; those who would demolish them overnight would erect greater injustices in their place. An absolute moral renewal of society can be attempted only by an absolute power which must inevitably destroy the moral life of man.[1]

Polanyi is here arguing for the integrity of the cultural life in its autonomy, which depends on its freedom from impositions by the tyranny of governments and of the majority. In the light of contemporary experience, Polanyi's position is obviously vulnerable, and its vulnerability may prevent us from seeing what is of value in it. So we might best begin with the vulnerability.

The rationale for elitism, which in the current radical view is the source of our present misery, is contained in the above passage. The political scientists who advised several American governments to undertake the Vietnam adventure constituted, after all, "a particular group of authoritative specialists perpetuating themselves by co-option." It may be possible to argue that this group of political scientists made corrupt use of their authority, and that the idea of perpetuation by co-option is in itself not invalidated. But such an argument I think is much too facile. For Polanyi's deductions about the political consequences of independent thought (for example, refraining from radical actions) suggest that the seeds of corruption are in Polanyi's politics. Here he is the spokesman for the confidence of the American and English clerisy in the existing institutional framework of American and English society. This confidence I think led to the current American hubris from which we are presently suffering.

The rationale for the confidence goes something like this. In America and England the intelligentsia has tended to regard its task as just and honorable, because the institutions it speaks for, in its view, are institutions that guarantee political liberty—for instance, the multi-party system, the electoral system, the checks against monolithic power in the balances created among the legislature, judiciary, and executive. Any deficiency in the institutions of a free society can be overcome in an orderly way, because the principle of constructive change is intrinsic to the institutions. What is curious about Polanyi's formulation, which I think represents the mental set of the intellectuals of the fifties, is that there is no explicit provision made for a dissenting group within the cultural leadership of a free society. The implication seems to be that necessary dissent will occur to the leadership as a whole, and that the required changes will follow as a matter of course. I suspect that the reason for this omission is that the intellectuals of the fifties were in recoil from their association with radical elitism, which for the most part took the form of Bolshevism. In recoiling from the association they adapted themselves uncritically to the cause of a "free society." The characteristic posture was to vaunt the virtues of that society's institutions rather than to criticize their inadequacies and failures (in the interest of the vitality of the institutions themselves). The virtues of a free society were insistently contrasted with the vices of a totalitarian society—more specifically, the preferability of life in Western democratic countries contrasted with life in the Soviet Union.

The truth in this contrast is in the fact that democratic institutions such as one finds in Western countries do provide political liberty missing in authoritarian socialist countries. The insistent way in which the point was made in the fifties was in part a function of the temptation of Marxism in its Stalinist version that the clerisy had experienced in the thirties, forties, and fifties. The temptation had to be overcome. There are of course less flattering explanations—such as the new seductions of power, status, and money offered by "a free society" to intellectuals willing to serve. But whatever the explanation, the fact of political liberty in Western countries diverted intellectuals from the necessary task of making a strenuous critique of their society's institutions.

The health of a modern democratic society is not in its capacity for vaunting its virtues, but in its capacity for developing an intelligent, moral, and effective dissenting clerisy that can help make necessary social changes. Lacking a constructive dissenting clerisy, a society tends to become an arena for polarization between a radical elite on the one hand, and the clerisy (and the majority) on the other. No moralizing about the totalitarian consequences of radical action is going to suppress permanently the radical impulse, because there is sufficient provocation in existing institutions for the radical impulse, and there is a spirit in some if not all men for radical revolt.

Polanyi's advocacy of change by carefully graded steps avoids a host of problems. If everyone in a society is careful, what will supply the impetus for change? There is no attention to the difference between the real consequences of a radical action, which may stimulate the dissenting clerisy, for instance, and the putative complete success of the action (on radical terms). He hedges a bit when he confirms his conservatism "on the whole." It would be interesting to know the exceptions. Do they occur when a society is losing its political liberty or when political liberty, as in America now, is not enough, that is, when more than political liberty is needed?

If political liberty means something, it means the freedom to follow one's *daimon,* even if it leads to antagonism toward established institutions. Any deliberate refraining from radical criticism is in a sense a contradiction to the project of sustaining independent thought. Moreover, the failure to encourage the spirit of dissent within the cultural leadership generally leads to a mindlessness about needed institutional change, and the possibility of the emergence of a disaffected radical elite is in direct proportion to the inadequacy of institutions to cope with existing problems and the failure of the clerisy to be in a critical relation to institutions.

So much for the serious vulnerability of Polanyi's position. But the project of sustaining independent disinterested thought is nonetheless important and possible. If we separate Polanyi's politics from his advocacy of cultural elitism (as I believe we can do), we can then accommodate to his view the kind of radical disinterestedness that can maintain the integrity of the cultural life and consequently the vitality and health of a free society.

II

The possibility of intellectual disinterestedness is of course at issue in the recent controversy—now muted, but still simmering—about the ideological character of the liberal university. I think it fair to say that whatever the differences between the exponents of the counterculture and the political radicals of anarchist persuasion might be, with significant exceptions they share a common political attitude toward the university. Whether in the interests of political activism or social service or the creation of new communal consciousness, the new militancy is by and large for politicizing the university, or rather repoliticizing it on its own terms.

The radical case for politicizing the university rests on the premise that the universities are political already. If the work of political science, sociology, and engineering is conducted not only under government auspices, but in the interest of formulating and executing government policy, it is disingenuous, so the radicals argue, for defenders of "academic freedom" to insist that the university remain free of politics.

Many radicals do not argue for a university that is free of politics because they are committed to a view that all thought is ideologically motivated and that the problem is to choose the right ideology, that is, one that fosters human values. As evidence of the political motivation of the universities they offer the fact that radical professors have difficulty getting or holding jobs either because of their activity or because the ideological assumptions of their commitment to a discipline (for example, Marxism) makes them uncongenial colleagues in the established departments.

The radical case rests largely on the character of the social sciences (in particular, political science). The evidence of subordination of the intellectual enterprise to government purposes is extensive. One must, however, distinguish among disciplines—for example, between political science on the one hand, and the study of literature or philosophy or mathematics on the other hand. There is doubtless an ideological component in all fields of study, but the ideological component does not necessarily make for servile scholarship, as any Marxist historian, for instance, would be quick to agree. It is an important distinction to make, because the issue is as much the extent and character of the politicization as the fact that the university is already politicized. If one can recite a long list of academic departments that are insubordinate to the political purposes of the American government, the argument about the inevitability of a politicized university becomes more difficult to make. The difficulty is generally avoided by those making the argument when they tend to identify the university with the social sciences and technology.* Thus a recent Marxist critic makes a strong case against existing departments of social science, but then addresses himself to the question of radically transforming the university as if social science were the prototype of all academic disciplines—a proposition that must be demonstrated,

---

* The problem with technological departments is not so much their ideology as their lack of ideology—that is, their capacity to serve the interests of any party.

not simply assumed.[2] All of this does not deny the problem of the social sciences and engineering.

Whatever the truth of the radical perception of the actual political character of the university, I would argue that there exists an element of bad faith in the desire of many radicals for a politicized university. The radicals justly charge their adversaries in political science departments with deforming the intellectual enterprise in the interests of an imperialist ideology, thereby implying their own commitment to genuine intellectual values. But radicals too often show little interest in intellectual values, which, after all, are by definition ideologically suspect. This judgment does not apply to Marxists who have an intellectual discipline as well as an ideology (note the restrictive subordinate clause here) and argue persuasively that the university does not sufficiently accommodate studies from a Marxist point of view. One can easily imagine a department of history or political science oriented on Marxist lines that would be intellectually distinguished —for instance, a department consisting of people like Eric Hobsbawm, William Appleman Williams, and Eugene Genovese. Such a department might or might not discriminate against non-Marxist candidates for positions within the department, but if it were distinguished, it would discriminate between competent and incompetent Marxists, between the intelligent and the foolish. Such discrimination proceeds from the fact that the discipline has standards against which performances can be judged. I suspect, moreover, that a mark of a distinguished Marxist department might very well be its policy of nondiscrimination toward non-Marxist scholarship. One of the virtues of Eugene Genovese is that he refuses to degrade the idea of scholarship by valuing mediocre work that calls itself radical or Marxist and by disvaluing distinguished work written from a conservative or liberal perspective. Indeed, he has acknowledged that radical scholarship in historical writing about the American south is not yet at the same level as—and consequently must learn from —scholarship of different, even opposed ideological motivation.

Here the value of disinterestedness is very real. Granted the personal and even ideological character of knowledge there still remains the possibility of a dialectical openness to the adversary position. Polanyi recalls Kant's eloquent assertion that this openness is not simply in the interest of tolerance, but rather in the interest of liquidating the doubt that plagues every honest commitment to an intellectual position. "The root of these disturbances, which lie deep in the nature of human reason, must be removed. But how can we do so, unless we give it freedom, nay, nourishment, to send out shoots so that it may discover itself to our eyes, and that it may then be entirely destroyed? We must, therefore, bethink ourselves of objections which have never yet occurred to any opponent, and indeed lend him our weapons, and grant him the most favorable position which he could possibly desire. We have nothing to fear, but much to hope for; namely, that we may gain for ourselves a possession which can never be contested." [3] And if the doubt cannot be liquidated one is open to the possibility of obtaining new truth, perhaps even the truth of the adversary position. Nothing in the argument for personal knowledge works against the argument for a disinterested openness to the adversary position. Indeed, it is precisely the awareness that we are all persons in limited possession of knowledge that makes it necessary that we open ourselves to the knowledge of other persons. The openness is a guarantee of the insubordinate character of the intellectual process. It is the intellect's way of preserving its autonomy, which is as necessary to its integrity as the imagination's need to obey its *daimon,* whatever the consequences.*

What is generally troubling in the intellectual stance of many radicals in the academy is that with respect to their disaffection from their disciplines they are often without ideas or even a sense of problem. They often claim that the

---

* A similar situation should obtain in the artistic imagination. The supreme capability of the novelist or the dramatist, as Keats first remarked, is the negative capability, in which the antagonist as well as the protagonist is given his due.

lack or chaos of ideas is simply a consequence of beginning
something new, forgetting that every new beginning has at its
basis a positive idea of sufficient power and coherence so
that constructive work can begin. The feeling that something
new is necessary or desirable is not the same as being in possession of something new. What makes this insufficiency offensive is that any substantial criticism or doubt about their
enterprise is met by resentment, irritability, sometimes even
intimidation. The skeptic is probably a counterrevolutionary
anyway.*

One begins to develop ideas in refuting the adversary position. But this is not possible if one is not in a dialectical
relation to the adversary. In order to achieve this relation
there must be an effort to understand the adversary position
and what motivates it. The current "radical" view of the adversary tends to be Manichean; the adversary is evil, low-

* Thomas Kuhn's statement about the value of orthodoxy for the
revolutionary act in science can I think be extended to other fields,
with due allowances for differences among the disciplines. For instance, in some disciplines, particularly the humanities, the orthodox
paradigm or paradigms are insufficiently defined, a fact which weak-
ens, though does not undermine, the case for the orthodox paradigm
in those fields. "In the normal mode of discovery, even resistance to
change has a use. By ensuring that the paradigm will not be too easily surrendered, resistance guarantees that scientists will not be
lightly distracted and that anomalies that lead to change will pene-
trate existing knowledge to the core" (Kuhn, *The Structure of Scientific Revolutions*, p. 65). And again: "The source of resistance is the
assurance that the older paradigm will ultimately solve all its problems, that nature can be shoved into the box the paradigm provides.
Inevitably, at times of revolution, the assurance seems as stubborn
and pigheaded as it sometimes becomes. But it is also something
more. The same assurance is what makes normal or puzzle-solving
science possible. And it is only through normal science that the professional community of scientists succeeds, first in exploiting the potential scope and precision of the older paradigms and, then, in isolating the difficulty through the study of which a new paradigm may
emerge" (pp. 50–51). And on a simply negative relation to the
existing paradigm, Kuhn remarks: "To reject one paradigm without
simultaneously substituting another is to reject science itself" (p. 79).
Kuhn gives a succinct account (unwittingly to be sure) of one motive
of the present intellectual despair that has turned many against the
intellectual enterprise: "though history is unlikely to record their
names, some men have undoubtedly been driven to desert science
because of their inability to tolerate crisis" (p. 78).

minded, motivated by prestige, money, and so forth. Doubtless some or perhaps many people are moved by base motives, but as a class judgment this is either hysterical or dishonest. This sort of judgment is, I think, one source of that "revolutionary justice" that is indiscriminate and inhumane (if and when it gets power) in its treatment of the "adversary." Note I am not saying that there is no evil in the adversary position. I am saying that what is required in the way of moral and intellectual honesty is scrupulousness and generosity in understanding the adversary position. Here one might distinguish between an activist and an intellectual relation to the adversary. On the barricades the effort of understanding is very difficult, if not impossible. But in the sphere of intellect it is essential for the strengthening of one's position (so that what is being attacked is real). The consequence of indiscriminately mixing the intellectual and activist styles is fatal for the intellectual integrity of one's position.

Unfortunately, a habit of indiscriminate confrontation has been fostered—as if every cause has equal value. The justification of confrontation is that the object of attack is not simply intransigent but morally and intellectually intolerable. By giving a maximal definition of what is intolerable opinion or behavior, confrontation politics becomes authoritarian. It is the exceptional and not the characteristic situation in the universities that justifies confrontation politics. Academic programs committed to the developing of military hardware seem to me one such exception. The university should have the right to exercise its judgment and authority on the question of whether an activity fosters disinterestedness and intellectual values. When such activity involves the application of knowledge to society, the determination of whether the application is humane is relevant and appropriate. The reluctance of a university to exercise such judgment invites extreme pressure from the other side. We are no longer in a period of widespread confrontation politics, but the intellectual and moral issues have yet to be dealt with in a satisfactory way.

The state of radical knowledge about the world is not at

the point where radicals are justified in easily dismissing a dialectical relation to the adversary position. Radical scholarship of very high quality exists in the field of American history (for example, the work of William Appleman Williams), in revisionist history of the Cold War (for example, the work of Gabriel Kolko), and in other fields, but it is usually the work of people who were radical before the fashion. Those who have lately adopted the fashion naturally turn to invective because their radicalism is often without intellectual substance. The authority of the radical critique in the universities will depend in part on its willingness and capacity to make its case in intellectual terms.

It may be argued that this is the moment for political commitment rather than intellectual disinterestedness. But even as a temporary strategy, the radical position is of dubious value.

If Galbraith (among others) is right in his persuasive account of the technostructure in *The New Industrial State* then a major social task of the university is to help create humane goals for a society in which the Gross National Product has achieved the status of deity. Galbraith rightly values university dissent of recent years for having dramatized the necessity of creating such goals. But where will the inspiration for these goals come from? Doubtless from many sources, including political experience. Certainly one major source must be the cultural tradition. The cultural tradition may prove refractory to those who impatiently demand that it prove its political usefulness immediately. This impatience encourages a costly act of renunciation, for those who deny the value of the cultural tradition are committing an act of self-mutilation and self-impoverishment, which no movement of social change can afford. The Cartesian spirit of beginning at the beginning and looking only to the future is fine, if one has rich, clear, and distinct ideas to fill the void. And if one does have these ideas, the chances are that one owes a debt to the cultural past.

But I do not think that the movement for a new university

(or what the French leftists have called *université critique*) has been intended as a temporary strategy. University radicals have been after bigger game than the mere suspending of the normal operations of the university. They want to transform the very idea of what the normal operations should be. They have been proposing an idea of the university that is largely based on political activism and social service. Despite the apparent demise of the student movement that idea has in somewhat emasculated form remained alive in the rhetoric and in some cases the actions of university administrators.

The raison d'être of an academic community is its relation to intellectual and educational standards. If the university is conceived as a community for political activism or social service or personal fulfillment, the intellectual activity of the members of the community becomes less important than the contribution members make to the cause or the human quality they possess in the eyes of the community. If one has shared the pains and joys of political struggle with another person, how is it practically possible to overcome the feeling of solidarity in order to judge his intellectual competence in a discipline. And who would want to make such a judgment when the discipline or the profession is so little valued—especially in contrast with the great political and moral drama being enacted.

My argument against politicizing the university is not made in behalf of a belief that a university should or can be politically indifferent. Though I can sympathize with Robert Brustein's recent eloquent defense of academic disinterestedness,[4] I cannot endorse his suggestion that a community college be created, an institution parallel to academic institutions that would be exclusively devoted to political activism and social service and would keep politics out of the university. Even if such a scheme were realistic, it must be faulted on the grounds that it would inhibit the natural political potentiality of the university. There are moments when political action is the natural outcome of intellectual inquiry.

Counterinsurgency programs express the view that "the American interest" must be maintained in underdeveloped countries in which revolutionary movements develop; opposition to counterinsurgency programs proceeds naturally from a view of the immorality or irrationality of American intervention in the internal affairs of other countries. In either case, the political idea is not naturally confined to the realm of speculation. It is not the suppression of political activity or social service that is required, but the keeping alive of a variety of political impulses, so that among other things the reactive and critical character of the university can be preserved and developed. (It may not be fortuitous that the liberal university has been the center of resistance to American policy in Vietnam, whereas the politicized universities of the peoples' democracies in Eastern Europe have been so reticent about the Soviet invasion of Czechoslovakia.)

But beyond the matter of making the university hospitable to a variety of political points of view is the matter of the limits of the political or activist mode in the life of the university and of the general society. Cultural and political ideals are not necessarily incompatible, though they may often be in significant tension. There is everything to be gained by acknowledging or even cultivating the tension. It is, to be sure, hard to resist political indignation, even when much of it has become ritualistic and self-indulgent. But such resistance is necessary if we are to avoid a diminishing political conception of the university and of the cultural life as a whole.

Notes   Index

Notes

Relevance and the Authority of Culture

1. José Ortega y Gasset, "In Search of Goethe from Within," trans. Willard R. Trask in *The Dehumanization of Art and Other Writings on Art and Culture* (New York: Doubleday Anchor, 1956), pp. 125, 127.

2. J. Lough, ed., *The Encyclopedia of Diderot and D'Alembert: Selected Articles* (Cambridge: Cambridge University Press, 1954), p. 5.

3. Donald M. Frame, trans., *The Complete Essays of Montaigne* (Stanford: Stanford University Press, 1965), p. 821.

4. *Ibid.*, p. 455.

5. See Donald M. Frame, *Montaigne* (New York: Harcourt Brace), pp. 320–321.

6. J. C. Pilkington, trans., *The Confessions of St. Augustine* (New York: Citadel Press, 1943), p. 143

7. Eric Auerbach, *Mimesis* (Princeton: Princeton University Press, 1971), pp. 69–70.

8. Roger Ingpen and Walter E. Peck, eds., *The Complete Works of Percy Bysshe Shelley* in ten vols. (New York: Gordian Press, 1965), VII, 134.

9. J. S. Mill, *Autobiography* (Oxford: Oxford University Press, 1952), p. 125.

10. J. S. Mill, *Utilitarianism, Liberty and Representative Government* (New York: Dutton, 1950), p. 1.

11. *Ibid.*, p. 45.

12. See Raymond Williams, *Culture and Society* (New York: Columbia University Press, 1960), p. 125.

13. See Michael Goodwin, *Opinion in Nineteenth Century England* (Harmondsworth, Middlesex: A Pelican Book, 1952), p. 192.

14. Allen Grossman, "Teaching Literature in a Discredited Civilization" in *Massachusetts Review*, 10.3 (Summer 1969): 420.

15. *Ibid.*, pp. 427, 429.

16. *Ibid.*, p. 426.

Cultural Radicalism in America and England

1. Richard Hofstadter, *Anti-Intellectualism in American Life* (New York: Alfred Knopf, 1963), p. 47.

2. Theodore Roszak, *The Making of a Counter Culture* (New York: Doubleday Anchor, 1969), pp. 233–234. Copyright 1968, 1969 by Theodore Roszak. Quoted by permission of Doubleday.

3. *Ibid.*, pp. 218–219.

4. *Ibid.*, pp. 213–214.

5. Thomas Kuhn, *The Structure of Scientific Revolutions* (Chicago; University of Chicago Press, 1964), p. 171.

6. Roszak, *The Making of A Counter Culture*, p. 141.

7. *Ibid.*, p. 75.

8. *Ibid.*, p. 209n.

9. *Ibid.*, p. 291.

10. Lev Shestov, *Athens and Jerusalem*, trans. Bernard Martin (New York: Simon and Shuster, 1968), pp. 207–208.

11. Roszak, *The Making of a Counter Culture*, p. 55.

12. Daniel and Gabriel Cohn-Bendit, *Obsolete Communism: The Left Wing Alternative* (New York: McGraw Hill, 1969), quoted in Roszak, p. 293.

13. Philip Slater, *The Pursuit of Loneliness* (Boston: Beacon Press, 1970), pp. 90, 335.

14. Raymond Williams, *The Long Revolution* (New York: Columbia University Press, 1961), p. 319–320.

15. *Ibid.*, p. 335.

16. Richard Hoggart, *Speaking to Each Other*, 2 vols. (New York: Oxford University Press, 1970), II, p. 246.

17. *Ibid.*, I, pp. 76–77.

18. Raymond Williams, *Culture and Society* (New York: Columbia University, 1960), p. 125.

19. *Ibid.*, p. 225.

The Humanities and Personal Knowledge

1. T. S. Eliot, *The Use of Poetry and the Use of Criticism* (London: Faber and Faber, 1933), conclusion.
2. Northrop Frye, *The Anatomy of Criticism* (Princeton: Princeton University Press, 1957), pp. 16, 18, 27.
3. Lionel Trilling, *Beyond Culture* (New York: The Viking Press, 1965), p. 231.
4. Matthew Arnold, *Selected Essays* (London: Oxford University Press, 1964), pp. 55, 77.
5. Raymond Williams, *Culture and Society* (New York: Columbia University Press, 1960), p. 110.
6. John Henry Newman, *The Grammar of Assent* (New York: A Doubleday Image Book, 1955), pp. 251, 275, 276.
7. *Ibid.*, p. 283.
8. Charles Harrold, Introduction to *A Grammar of Assent* (New York: Longmans, Green, 1943), p. xiv.
9. Newman, *The Grammar of Assent*, p. 272.
10. *Ibid.*, pp. 293, 287.
11. *Ibid.*, p. 283.
12. Michael Polanyi, *Personal Knowledge* (Chicago: University of Chicago Press, 1960), p. 258.
13. *Ibid.*, p. 267.
14. Roland Barthès, *Essais critiques* (Paris: Editions de Seuil, 1964), p. 254.

Literary Study and Radicalism

1. Bruce Franklin, "Teaching Literature in the Higher Academies of the Empire" in *College English*, March 1970, pp. 548, 549, 550.
2. *Ibid.*, p. 555.
3. Frederick C. Crews, "Do Literary Studies Have an Ideology?" in *PMLA*, May 1970, p. 427.
4. *Ibid.*, pp. 427–428.
5. In William Van, O'Connor, ed., *Forms of Modern Fiction* (Minneapolis: University of Minnesota Press, 1948), pp. 9, 10.
6. James Goldberg, *Kenyon Review*, 127 (Summer 1969): 601.

7. John R. Harrison, *The Reactionaries* (London: Victor Gollancz, 1966), p. 15.

8. *Ibid.*, pp. 50–51.

High Culture and Democracy

1. Alexis de Tocqueville, *Democracy in America,* the Henry Reeve Text as revised by Frances Bowen, 2 vols. (New York: Alfred Knopf, 1945), II, 44.

2. Third Dialogue, *Dialogues Philosophiques,* quoted in Paul Lidsky, *Les Ecrivains contre la commune* (Paris: Maspero, 1970), pp. 30–31, my translation.

3. Alexander Herzen, *From the Other Shore,* trans. Richard Wollheim (London: Weidenfeld and Nicolson, 1956), p. 116.

4. Tocqueville, *Democracy in America,* II, 50.

5. Herzen, *From the Other Shore,* pp. 63–64.

6. Theodore Roszak, *The Making of a Counter Culture* (New York: Doubleday Anchor, 1969), pp. 233–234.

7. *Culture and Anarchy,* ed. J. Dover Wilson (Cambridge: at the University Press, 1957), p. 70.

8. Tocqueville, *Democracy in America,* II, 39.

Utopia and the Irony of History

1. Thomas More, *Utopia,* trans. Paul Turner (Baltimore: Penguin Book, 1967), p. 131.

2. Stendhal, *The Charterhouse of Parma,* trans. C. K. Scott Moncrieff (New York: Liveright, 1944) p. 20.

3. *Ibid.,* p. 4.

4. Alexis de Tocqueville, *The Old Regime and the French Revolution,* trans. Stuart Gilbert (Garden City, New York: Doubleday Anchor Books, 1955), pp. 140 and 141.

5. Alexis de Tocqueville, *Recollections of 1848,* trans. Alexander Teixeira de Mattos, ed. J. P. Mayer (New York: Columbia University Press, 1949), p. 158.

6. Alexander Herzen, *From the Other Shore* (London: Weidenfeld and Nicolson, 1956), p. 64.

7. Friedrich Engels, *Socialism: Scientific and Utopian* in

Lewis S. Feuer, *Marx and Engels: Basic Writings* (New York: Doubleday Anchor, 1959), pp. 73–74, 69.

8. *Ibid.*, p. 74.

9. Edmund Burke, *Reflections on the French Revolution* (New York: Rinehart and Winston, 1962), p. 39.

10. Karl Marx, *The Eighteenth Brumaire of Louis Napoleon,* in Karl Marx and Frederick Engels, *Selected Works in Two Volumes,* I (Moscow: Foreign Languages Publishing House, 1951), 225.

11. *Ibid.*, p. 267.

12. *Ibid.*, p. 226.

13. Marx, *The Class Struggles in France,* in Feuer, *The Basic Writings,* p. 289.

14. *Ibid.*, p. 281.

15. Harold Rosenberg, *The Tradition of the New* (New York: McGraw Hill, 1965), p. 168.

16. Engels, *Introduction to the Civil War in France,* in Feuer, *The Basic Writings,* p. 358.

17. Rosenberg, *The Tradition of the New,* p. 169.

18. Alexander Herzen, *Lettres de France et D'Italie* (Geneve, 1871), Lettre XI, p. 254 (my translation).

19. Gustave Flaubert, *The Sentimental Education* (New York: New Directions, 1957), p. 510.

20. Hannah Arendt, *On Revolution* (New York: Viking, 1963), p. 52.

21. George Kateb, *Utopia and Its Enemies* (Glencoe, Illinois: Free Press, 1963), p. 199.

22. Fyodor Dostoevsky, *Notes from the Underground,* trans. Andrew R. MacAndrew (New York: NAL, 1961), p. 110.

23. More, *Utopia,* pp. 92–93.

24. Dostoevsky, *Notes from the Underground,* p. 203.

25. Eugene Zamiatin, *We,* trans. Gregory Zilborg (New York: E. P. Dutton, 1924), p. 59.

26. *Ibid.*, pp. 127–128.

27. "Literature, Entropy and Revolution," translated by Walter N. Vickery in *Partisan Review,* nos. 3–4, 1961, p. 378.

28. George Orwell, *1984* (London: Secker and Warburg, 1949), p. 250.

29. Judith Shklar, *After Utopia* (Princeton: Princeton University Press, 1958), pp. 245 f.

30. "Gerontion" in T. S. Eliot, *Collected Poems, 1909–50* (New York: Harcourt Brace), p. 22. Quoted by permission of Harcourt Brace Jovanovich and Faber and Faber.

31. Daniel Cohn-Bendit, *The French Student Revolt,* trans. B. R. Brewster (New York: Hill and Wang, 1968), p. 78.

32. Marx, *The Eighteenth Brumaire*, p. 301.
33. Herbert Marcuse, *Eros and Civilization* (Boston: Beacon Press, 1955), p. 57.
34. Zamiatin, *We*, p. 27.
35. *Ibid.*, pp. 22–23.
36. *Ibid.*, p. 151.

The Imagination and the Temptations of Politics

1. Friedrich Schiller, *On the Aesthetic Education of Man*, ed. and trans. Elizabeth M. Wilkinson and L. A. Willoughby (Oxford: Clarendon Press, 1967), p. 9. Quoted by permission of The Clarendon Press, Oxford.
2. *Ibid.*, p. 7.
3. *Ibid.*, p. 21.
4. *Ibid.*, p. 55.
5. *Ibid.*, p. 59.
6. *Ibid.*, p. 13.
7. *Ibid.*, p. 25.
8. *Ibid.*, pp. 169, 91, 93, 211, 219.
9. *Ibid.*, p. 213.
10. *Ibid.*, p. 219.
11. R. H. Super, ed., *The Complete Prose Works of Matthew Arnold*, 6 vols. (Ann Arbor: The University of Michigan Press, 1962), II, 324.
12. André Breton, *Manifestoes of Surrealism*, trans. Richard Seaver and Helen R. Lane (Ann Arbor: The University of Michigan Press, 1969), pp. 235–236.
13. *Ibid.*, p. 114.
14. J. H. Matthews, *Surrealist Poetry in France* (Syracuse: Syracuse University Press, 1969), p. 106. Quoted by permission.
15. Breton, *Manifestoes of Surrealism*, pp. 4–5.
16. *Ibid.*, pp. 4, 10, 18.
17. Herbert Read, ed., *Surrealism* (New York: Harcourt Brace, 1936), p. 96.
18. Matthews, *Surrealist Poetry in France*, pp. 38–39.
19. *Ibid.*, p. 34. My translation.
20. From *Corps Perdu*. J. H. Matthews, *An Anthology of French Surrealist Poetry* (London: University of London Press, 1966), pp. 79–80. My translation.
21. André Breton, "Legitimate Defense" (September 1926), in Maurice Nadeau, *The History of Surrealism*, trans. Richard Howard (London: Jonathan Cape, 1964), p. 252.

22. Breton, *Manifestoes*, p. 47.

23. Matthews, *Surrealist Poetry in France*, p. 221.

24. Herbert Marcuse, *Eros and Civilization* (Boston: Beacon Press, 1955), p. 162.

25. Norman O. Brown, "A Reply to Marcuse," *Commentary*, March 1967, p. 83.

26. Theodore Roszak, *The Making of a Counter Culture* (New York: Doubleday Anchor, 1969), p. 120.

27. Lionel Trilling, "Authenticity and the Modern Unconscious" in *Commentary* (September 1971), p. 50. This essay is Chapter VI in Trilling's *Sincerity and Authenticity* (Cambridge: Harvard University Press, and London: Oxford University Press, 1972).

28. Introduction to "The Grand Inquisitor" in *Phoenix: The Posthumous Papers of D. H. Lawrence,* ed. E. D. MacDonald (London: Heinemann, 1961), p. 290.

29. Marinetti, "The Manifesto of Futurism." Translation in James Joll, *Three Intellectuals in Politics* (New York: Pantheon Books, 1960), pp. 181–184. Quoted by permission of Pantheon Books, a Division of Random House.

30. "The Cloud in Trousers," trans. George Reavey in Vladimir Mayakovsky, *The Bedbug and Selected Poetry,* ed. Patricia Blake (New York: Meridian, 1960), pp. 71, 75, 81, 87. Copyright © 1960 by The World Publishing Company. Reprinted by permission of The World Publishing Company.

31. Friedrich Nietzsche, *Human All Too Human,* 2 vols. Translated by Paul V. Cohn and Helen Zimmern (London and Edinburgh: J. N. Foulis, 1910), II, 199.

32. W. B. Yeats, *The Collected Poems of W. B. Yeats* (New York: Macmillan, 1958), p. 206. Quoted by permission of M. B. Yeats; the Macmillan Company, New York; and the Macmillan Companies of London and Canada.

33. Tuscan Diary, 1898. Quoted in Eric Heller, *The Disinherited Mind* (Harmondsworth, Middlesex: Penguin Books, 1961), p. 121.

Ideology and Disinterestedness

1. Michael Polanyi, *Personal Knowledge* (Chicago: University of Chicago Press, 1960), pp. 244, 245.

2. Cf. David Horowitz, "Social Science or Ideology" in *Social Policy* (September, October 1970), pp. 30–36.

3. Quoted in Polanyi, *Personal Knowledge,* p. 270, from Kant's *Critique of Pure Reason.*

4. Robert Brustein, "The Decline of Professionalism" in *Modern Occasions* (Fall 1970), pp. 79–86; especially p. 86.

Index